Bob Dylan,
Bruce Springsteen,
& Rock Fiction

Bob Dylan, Bruce Springsteen, & Rock Fiction

Franny Hatch, Bob Dylan's friend

To order additional copies of this book, contact:
Xlibris
844-714-8691
www.Xlibris.com
Orders@Xlibris.com
842408

Dedicated to Bob Dylan, super stage legend
rocker extraordinaire, and my friend

Super-Stage Legend Rockers

Bob Dylan

"The magic of Dylan will continue," a noted newspaper proclaimed once. Bob Dylan said that meant a lot to him and was special to him as he went through his European tour, *Bob Dylan—Family & Friends*, for the past couple of years and currently.

"The hero will be me," Bob Dylan said, quoting a rock song.

Bob Dylan, the voice of all times, has seen "The Times They Are A-Changin'."

The legalization of recreational marijuana in eighteen states has happened with a lot of help from Bob Dylan and his super-stage legend rocker buddies like Bruce Springsteen, James Taylor, and Micki Jagger.

"Barack Obama, when he was president, I can acknowledge for telling me the best way to do legalization was probably to go state by state," said Bob Dylan.

Some of the states where recreational marijuana is legal include Colorado, California, Oregon, Washington state, Nevada, Alaska, Michigan, Vermont, Maine, Rhode Island, and also Washington, D.C.

This year, 2020, the recent edition of *Rolling Stone* featured Bob Dylan's first original song in years, "Murder Most Foul," in which the Nobel and Pulitzer prize-winning Bard of Rock told of a look at U.S. history centering on JFK and others, and also the influence of music to take rockers and others through bad things.

Last year's *Bob Dylan—Family & Friends* tour led the band through Norway, Finland, Sweden, Hamberg, Germany, where King Charles discovered the Beatles, other cities in Germany, the United Kingdom, including Hyde Park, London, and the U.S.

Bob Dylan has been writing rock songs and working with his band, except for Kris Kristofferson, because "we're already rehearsed. He's been down here, and we know each other's styles."

Kris Kristofferson ("Sunday Morning Comin' Down") has appeared in the front row on stage in many other Bob Dylan concerts.

On tour with Bob Dylan in *Bob Dylan—Family & Friends*, among others, are also Neil Young ("Sugar Mountain") and G. Jagger.

Micki Jagger has said he will help all fourteen of his kids get going on their stage careers.

Many of the songs Bob Dylan wrote are meant to be introduced in concert because Bob Dylan likes to "spring them on the rockers in his concerts."

Bob Dylan was friendly, as he always is.

"I've been painting a little—not a lot," Bob Dylan said, as he and I both remembered a painting of his which had been in *Rolling Stone*: a prominent railroad track meandering through town, with off in the distance, a cool bright red/orange glittering sunset.

Bob Dylan continued: "I've been seeing people. You know them— Bruce Springsteen every day, Paul McCartney, James Taylor, Santana, Micki Jagger, and my band mates. I've also seen David Crosby, Clint Eastwood, Jann Wenner (*Rolling Stone*), John Fogarty, Daniel Lanoi (music producer), and Ronnie Howard. I've been spending a lot of time jamming." "What new songs have you done?" he was asked.

"I think them up all the time, sometimes when I'm jamming. Kris Kristofferson does too," the affectionate Bard said.

Bob Dylan, poet laureate of rock, made history by becoming the only singer-songwriter to win a Nobel Prize.

Knowing Bob Dylan is like knowing Shakespeare, TV broadcasters have said.

"I respond to love," Bob Dylan also said.

Bob Dylan has over six hundred original compositions and many awards, including two Oscars, eleven Grammies, and numerous music awards, a Presidential Medal of Freedom, a Pulitzer Prize, a Nobel, and a Kennedy Center Award. He has also appeared in several films and videos, including his first movie, *Pat Garrett and Billy the Kid*, in which he played Alias, and Kris Kristofferson portrayed Billy the Kid. In addition, Bob Dylan now produces his albums and owns a radio station.

Bob Dylan had marveled the world—loved by his rocker friends everywhere, including leaders of the U.S. and other countries, Jimmy Carter, Micki Jagger, King Charles, Prince Will, Paul McCartney, Ron Woods, Bruce Springsteen, James Taylor, Mark Knopfler, David Crosby, Santana, and rockers everywhere who flock to his concerts and get his albums like friends, many in leather jackets, T-shirts, and jeans and sandals or boots.

"What do you use for inspiration?" Bob Dylan was asked.

The Bard was calm, in a new light blue T-shirt, jean shorts, and tennis shoes with orange accents. "My inspiration comes from inside," the super-stage legend rocker said. "Words are always first. Music comes from inside."

"I use palm muting, and I play like Bruce Springsteen, who uses it." (Springsteen likes it because it's kind of a gutsy, low-down sound, Bruce Springsteen said.)

Bob Dylan uses Gibson and Fender electric guitars and Fender acoustic guitars on stage. He uses Marshall amps. "They're the best," he said, and ended his answer with, "I don't want to give away all my secrets."

"What is most inspirational about Bob Dylan?" Paul McCartney was asked as he came down in a black leather jacket and jeans.

"He thinks, he reads, he assimilates, he is wise, and I care about him," Paul McCartney said. "We changed American history."

Jimmy Carter, another of Bob Dylan's friends, first met Bob Dylan backstage at one of his rock concerts.

"His friends are inspirational—they love him," Jimmy Carter said, "including Micki Jagger and King Charles. They'd do anything they can to save America. And Bob Dylan never gives up."

Bob Dylan's songs, "All Along the Watch Tower" and "Masters of War," have the same theme—keeping America safe, Bob Dylan said.

Both Bob Dylan and Jimmy Carter are interested in the legalization of marijuana. After Oregon and Alaska put legalization of recreational pot on the ballot in 2014 (and made it), Jimmy Carter said, "I didn't have anything to do with that. Or I won't say I did."

Jimmy Carter's favorite Bob Dylan songs are "Everybody Must Get Stoned," ("Everybody likes that one," Carter said) and "All Along the Watch Tower" ("for obvious reasons").

Among the U.S. presidents, Bob Dylan has known Bill Clinton and Ronald Reagan.

"I first met Barack Obama when he placed the Medal of Freedom on me," Bob Dylan said.

Bob Dylan lived in a complex of cabins at Joshua Tree, California, with Reagan and other rock people from Woodstock when Reagan was president.

"Reagan wanted everyone to know he loved California, and he loved his rockers," Bob Dylan said.

Bruce Springsteen feels what is most important about Bob Dylan is "his straightforwardness; he speaks from the street. He's a large voice. A lot of people relate to him."

Micki Jagger rock-sings songs on the radio about Bob Dylan:

"Bobbee is successful" or
"Bob Dylan, I love you so (as a friend)
I'm famous
And so are you!"

What David Crosby finds most inspirational about Bob Dylan is he knows everything or knows how to find out.

"Everybody Must Get Stoned" is his favorite Bard song. "I've gotten stoned enough times to that one," Crosby said.

Bob Dylan came out in a medium green jacket and jeans to see me and to answer questions about his albums.

"What was the concept of the *Freewheelin' Bob Dylan* album," the super-stage legend rocker was asked.

"Bob Dylan's on a roll," he answered.

The *Infidels* album: "I like infidels or people who are out of sync. That's what it was about."

Knocked Out Loaded: "I had a lot of fun doing that, and obviously it's in there—with me and my friends."

Down in the Groove: "When I'm happy, I'm in the groove."

When asked how he liked working with Daniel Lanoi, who produced some of his albums, Bob Dylan said, "I loved it. He's great."

When asked if anyone gave him ideas he used for an album, the likable Bard said, "Not a lot, but it's private."

"How do you come up with the theme song and songs for a movie?" Bob Dylan was asked.

"I watched the movie a few times, thought, and wrote. Writing is absolute. I don't do more than once. I like it, always," the prolific singer/songwriter noted.

Bob Dylan was then asked about more albums.

Street Legal: "About marijuana," he said.

"*Real Live* was about one of my concerts," Bob Dylan said.

"*Oh Mercy* concerned things I might need to swear over. It's a mild one."

"*Self Portrait* is about me, and I like me," Bob Dylan said.

"*Dylan* is the same," he reiterated.

"*Slow Train Coming* concerns religion," he said.

Tempest was once explained on the internet as his last album. Then, soon after, three new albums were listed: *My New Morning* (2014), *Bob Dylan—The Warehouse* (2014), and *Another Self Portrait*.

"*Tempest* is not my last—I go on and on," Bob Dylan said.

Since then, Bob Dylan has come out with other new albums: *Shadows in the Night* (2015), *Fallen Angels* (2016), and *Triplicate* (2017). Another album was listed after that: *Bob Dylan & The New Folk Movement*.

"I love all my awards," Bob Dylan said. In addition to those already mentioned, Bob Dylan received France's Legion of Honor, the *Commandeur des Artset des Lettres*, from the Ministry of Culture in Paris. He also received honorary doctorates from Princeton and the

University of St. Andrews (Scotland). The Pulitzer Prize and the Nobel were his favorite awards "because no other rocker has one."

Bob Dylan has also been crowned with achievements in the Rock 'N Roll Hall of Fame (award given by Bruce Springsteen), the Songwriters Hall of Fame, and the Nashville Songwriters Hall of Fame.

He also got the Founders Award from ASCAP, Beverly Hills (American Society of Composers, Authors, and Publishers).

In 1985, Bob Dylan had a worldwide audience exceeding one billion.

"I'm a singer-songwriter," Bob Dylan explained. "When I see my song has a good effect on someone, I feel good inside."

Bob Dylan likes his friends to know each other. He has a radio station somewhere in the U.S.—he didn't say where— which he uses to get his and other super-stage legend rockers on, like Paul McCartney, Bruce Springsteen, James Taylor, Micki Jagger, and the Rolling Stones.

When asked what types of audiences he liked best, the guitar-totin' harmonica blowin' keyboardist and singer Bob Dylan said, "any that liked me, which was most of them usually."

The best stages, Bob Dylan feels, "are those with a good view for the audience. There were not a lot of wrap-arounds, and for those in the back of a stage like that, it was the pits." Stage size was not very important, Bob Dylan remarked.

When asked how he established good relations with amphitheater managers like Mikey or Paul Nedermiere or Susan, or the Nederlanders (amphitheater and theater entrepreneurs), the super-stage legend rocker answered, "I found them likeable, and didn't try too hard."

The Nederlanders—James L. (concerts) and James M. (theater play producer and now writing a book, a *Star Wars* sequel)—and part of the Nederlander organization know Bob Dylan very well.

Mikey is a Nederlander executive and is now a Nederlander partner.

Dylan got to be friends with the friendly Nederlanders by "just being around them."

In relating to his rock music, Bob Dylan, said his favorite songs are "all of them. I have no favorites. I set up songs for an area."

Bob Dylan reflected on his anecdotes and memories in making some of his albums, (*Tempest*, *Lost on the River*, the new *Basement Tapes*), and *Bob Dylan—The Warehouse*: "I wanted traces of me for posterity and people to love me."

"It was the same for recording *Another Self Portrait*," Bob Dylan said, adding, "And I left good memories."

Bob Dylan jams with Paul Simon "whenever he's around."

Of a few of his other friends, the Bard mentioned, "Paul McCartney is a good buddy, Santana cares, Bruce Springsteen is close to me, James Taylor is a love (loved friend), Micki Jagger is one hell of a man, and the Rolling Stones, the same—one hell of a group. Ringo Starr—I like him."

Besides all the rockers Bob Dylan has partied with, like Crosby, Stills, and Nash, Paul Simon, Eric Clapton, James Taylor, Bruce Springsteen, Micki Jagger, Cher, and Paul McCartney, he has also partied with Clint Eastwood, Martin Scorsese, David Geffin, Stephen Spielberg, Ronnie Howard, and Jane Fonda.

Bob Dylan explained his songs: "My style of music is unique. The most fortunate person happens on it. It changes their life."

"Let It Be Me"—one of my favorites," Bob Dylan said. "It means what it says—I want to be the one."

"For 'When I Paint My Masterpiece,' I like to draw and paint. I have books of all or some drawings I did, and some art in *Rolling Stone*," he shared. "'Don't Think Twice, It's All Right' means everything's gonna be OK."

"'Blowin' in the Wind' is one of my favorite songs because Dave Ronk, a musician I hold in esteem, commented on it. He said, 'What the heck is blowin' in the wind?'" Bob Dylan recalled.

"For 'The Times They Are A-Changin', I've talked about it too much. OK, it's too hard. Let's change some things," he said. "In 'Mr. Tamborine Man,' I want to party. That's about it. For 'Forever Young,' that's easy. Stay forever young. Be a rocker, some folks say. I agree."

"'All I Really Wanta Do' is one of my favorites. Friendship is important. So is love," he said. "'Come In Through My Window' means be friends with me."

"'Trust Yourself' means what it says. That's why everyone likes it," Bob Dylan explained.

Bruce Springsteen

Bruce Springsteen has done everything from visiting the president to delighting rockers everywhere.

A day before the presidential election, Bruce Springsteen was with President Barack Obama, rocking for him while Obama gave speeches.

"No retreat, no surrender," sang the super-stage legend Springsteen.

That night, the Boss and the President got on Air Force One for Bruce's first flight on it.

"Pretty cool," Springsteen rocked.

The next day, when Barack Obama won, after he gave his acceptance speech, and confetti soared above the president, the Boss's soundtrack welled up, and the crowd got his song: "We take care of our own."

Less than a few weeks earlier, Taylor Swift, appearing on the *Ellen* TV show, showed a video of Bruce Springsteen playing one of her guitars that he had autographed for her at her request.

Taylor Swift said he had surprised her by calling her people when she had a show that night, announcing he would be on her show that night, and going to meet her at a "meet and greet."

"I really liked her a lot," the Boss said, coming to see me the third time in three months, this time wearing a black sports jacket over a tan sweater, black slacks, thin black socks, and cool Gentleman's Quarterly-style slip-on shoes. It was a few days before Thanksgiving.

I met Bruce Springsteen in California.

"What's going on, Bruce?"

Bruce Springsteen: "I'm working on a new album with old rock 'n' roll and blues songs looked at to find out what produces, as far as a concept. It might be back to the blues or something like that. One song is called 'ROBO,' which means 'Rock On Or Back Off.' It's rock because a lot of stuff out today is so simple. I'm just trying to bring back the blues—that's where rock started. We've got about half of the songs done for the album."

"Do you use palm muting, arpeggios, or string skipping?"

Bruce Springsteen: "I use a lot of palm muting. It's kind of a gutsy, low-down sound. Other than that, not a lot 'cause I like it raw."

"What kind of guitars do you use on stage?"

Bruce Springsteen: "Mostly Gibson guitars. If I'm not playing Gibson, then Fender. I use Marshall amps, just because it's old school and is animal sound and down and dirty,"

"What other artists do you like?"

Bruce Springsteen: Carlos Santana and Van Halen. I could name a bunch more, but a few are Black Sabbath, Ted Nugent, and go back to the old-time blues—Howling Wolf, B.B. King—and the ultimate one who started it all, Robert Johnson."

"Do you like Bob Dylan?"

Bruce Springsteen: "He's very smart. And I like his lyrics."

"Do you like James Taylor?"

Bruce Springsteen: "Oh yeah. He's a cool guy. I like his songs too."

"What do you use for inspiration?"

Bruce Springsteen: "Life experiences—any and all. It has to come from the soul."

"When composing, which do you write first: the music or the words?"

Bruce Springsteen: "That's a good one. It's a combo. When I'm composing some songs, I find words first. Some, I feel the melody and play it, and try to put it in words later. There's no set formula."

"Do you memorize the songs after you've written them, and then video-record them, or write them down as sheet music?"

Bruce Springsteen: "Memorize. I never write it down."

"Tell us about your European tour."

"I rocked the stage in France, Italy, Germany, Liverpool in Great Britain (where the Beatles come from), Austria, Finland, Denmark, Czechoslavakia, and Yugoslavia. It was a wild trip. But it went smoothly. Those trips are rare."

Bob Dylan, Bruce Springsteen, Jane Fonda, and Cher Racing

Chapter 1

Bob Dylan watched as his birthday present to Franny came about.

Jane Fonda, a good friend of Bob Dylan's, was out where Franny was shopping.

They said hi. Jane Fonda was wearing a rolled-up sleeveless and tied at the hem yellow and black plaid shirt—large plaid—and jeans.

Theater James Nederlander was out there in a green and navy striped shirt and jeans and said hi several times.

*   *   *

"I could be in a movie you're doing about Cher. I'm very cool and intricate like Cher," Jane Fonda said.

Bruce Springsteen came in and sat down between Franny and Bob Dylan.

"That was Bobbee's birthday present to you—a new book and love from his friends," Bruce Springsteen said to Franny.

Bobbee Dylan and Franny and Bruce Springsteen all hugged.

Jane Fonda and Theater James Nederlander cheered.

Jane Fonda said, "I've been looking for a new movie to do that's fun and adventurous. I like Cher that you're doing, Franny. Bob Dylan told me about it, and the Bard said he wanted to give you a birthday present with fun people to write another movie."

"Jane Fonda likes to have fun," Bob Dylan said.

"Bob Dylan does too," Jane Fonda said.

"Bob Dylan gives wonderful birthday presents," Bruce Springsteen said.

"I love you, Bobbee," Franny said.

*   *   *

"Beat Generation"

Bob Dylan stood on stage at Mikey's Nederlander amphitheater concert and rocked out his new song, "The Beat Generation."

> We're the Beat Generation.
> We Never Get Old
> We're Not S_____ C_____
> We're the Beat Generation.
> We're the Beat Generation
> Yeah
> We're the Beat Generation!

The rockers in the concert audience—everyone, every generation—went wild with joy.

Bob Dylan and his band and the rockers were on TV that night.

"We're the Beat Generation"

Jane Fonda and Cher were shown in the rocker audience, with Bob Dylan on stage.

*   *   *

"I'm going to have fun today, baby," Bob Dylan said to Franny.

Bob Dylan came out on stage to a full house, packed with rockers and other super-stage legend rockers.

Jane Fonda and Cher were in the rocker audience.

King Charles and Prince Will were in the audience.

The three Nederlanders and Mikey cheered.
Bob Dylan dedicated a song to Franny:

I Love You, Baby
You're Wonderful
I Want Your Love

James Taylor and crew were there.
Bruce Springsteen was there.
David Crosby was there.
Bob Dylan rocked on.

First Concert

My concert was wonderful
My concert was wonderful
Yay, Baby!

"All my fans loved me. I have 150 letters and notes to read tomorrow. Mikey hasn't counted, but he said it looks like at least 150," Bob Dylan said to Franny.

Chapter 2

"I named all my kids," Micki Jagger said to Bob Dylan. "Except for Karis. Her mother named her. You like Karis?"

"Sure. I feel it's great," Bob Dylan said.

"I feel that way too. Pretty cool," Micki Jagger said.

"Everything about you is wonderful. I love you, baby," Bob Dylan said to Franny.

"I love you, Bobbee," Franny said.

They kissed.

Soon Bob Dylan, Micki Jagger, and Franny were talking to Bruce Springsteen, James Taylor, Cher, Jane Fonda, Jann Wenner, and Clint Eastwood.

"What are the names of your other kids, Micki Jagger?" Jane Fonda asked.

"Jade, Jasmine, Kim, Elizabeth, James, G. Jagger, Brad, Tori, Wolfgang, Georgia-May, Gabriel, Liv Tyler, and Lucas," Micki Jagger said.

"Cool, Micki Jagger. Those are great names," Bruce Springsteen said.

"Hey, cool, matey!" Micki Jagger said.

*   *   *

Franny went into the editor/publisher's office and instantly noticed the surroundings.

The lobby was well-furnished, with a polished brown desk and several chairs.

"Hello, Franny," the editor, Tyrone, said, greeting her immediately as he stepped out of his office.

"Hi, Tyrone," Franny said.

They went into Tyrone's office.

"I'd like an article on six people," Tyrone said. "Bob Dylan, Jane Fonda, Cher, Bruce Springsteen, James Taylor, and Micki Jagger. I understand Jane Fonda's going to do a movie with all those rockers."

"What's the title?" Franny asked.

"Undecided as yet. They're going to have a lot of stage scenes of concerts, and Jane Fonda's relationship with Bob Dylan, James Taylor, Cher, Bruce Springsteen, and Micki Jagger, and basically the whole cool rocker world," Tyrone said.

"And one publisher/editor is going to be in the movie, Jann Wenner, publisher and founder of *Rolling Stone*. Get him in the article too, Franny, OK? Here's a list of all their phone numbers," Tyrone added.

"Cool," Franny said. "I love rock, and Bob Dylan's my best friend, and he introduced me to all those people."

"Great," Tyrone said. "I know Bob Dylan loves you, and you love him, and that's why I felt you'd be perfect to do the article. I know Jann Wenner, and he was conveying the movie news to me."

"That's cool, Tyrone," Franny said. "This is exciting. I'll get right on it."

"Great. How about two weeks from today, on Friday afternoon, the twentieth of August?" Tyrone said.

"Great. Bob Dylan has two concerts in Kansas City this week," Franny said. "I'll find out about going and call the others and find out about their concerts."

"I can go with you," Tyrone said. "I've got the concert schedules of all of them, and Bruce Springsteen is tomorrow night. I'll pick you up, and we'll go together. Of course, you and I will get press passes."

"Far out," Franny said. "Bob Dylan is in concert Sunday night."

"That's on my list," Tyrone said. "We'll get to everyone's concert in two weeks easy: James Taylor, Micki Jagger, the Rolling Stones, Cher, and Bruce Springsteen."

"I'll find out if Jane Fonda is going to any of those concerts we are," Franny said.

"Super," Tyrone said. "I'll meet you at 6:30 on concert nights. Here's a list, and we'll go on over."

"Great. It'll be worthwhile to view all those concerts. I love rock music and Bob Dylan and super-stage legend rockers and everything they're doing," Franny said.

The secretary, Venna, knocked on the door. "Bob Dylan is here, and he wants to be with both of you," she said.

Tyrone greeted Bob Dylan at the door. "Hi, Bob Dylan."

"Bobbee!" Franny said.

Bob Dylan came in, hugged, and kissed his best friend, Franny. Bob Dylan was her best friend.

Tyrone gave them the conference room so Franny could interview Bob Dylan, while Tyrone set up and took pictures as the Bard and Franny did the interview.

*   *   *

Bob Dylan was magnificent in both pictures and quotes that came out for the article, which came out in next month's edition of *Rock On!* The *Rolling Stone* reprinted it.

"I love being magnificent," Bob Dylan said to Franny.

*   *   *

"If you write like that," Jann Wenner told Franny, "It's not because Bob Dylan is being interviewed; it's because he is loved."

Chapter 3

On the day after Bob Dylan's fourth summer concert, which had been fantastic, the rockers had been fantastic and loved Bob Dylan and his music.

And I Would Not Feel So All Alone
Everybody Must Get Stoned

Bob Dylan, Neil Young, and Kris Kristofferson rocked out.

Clint Eastwood discussed with Lorraine Chaney, Jane Fonda, and Cher: "Charles Schumer, Senate Majority Leader, has introduced a bill, the *Cannabis Administrative and Opportunity Act*, which would legalize recreational marijuana at the federal level. (A similar bill had passed in the House.) If Charles Schumer's Senate Cannabis bill passed, it would go for approval to the president.

"Bob Dylan and his super-stage legend rocker friends have been working on the legalization of recreational marijuana for a long time. Barack Obama had advised Bob Dylan that going state by state in State's Rights would be the best way to get legalized.

"Now, eighteen states have legalized recreational cannabis."

"There's two ways marijuana can be legalized at the federal level," Clint Eastwood said. "One is federally—through that process going on."

"What's the other one?" Jane Fonda asked.

"If a certain percentage of states agree to legalization—I forget the percentage—but it works out to thirty-eight anyway," Clint Eastwood said. "If that happens—either way—it's a go for legalization."

"Hey, great," Jane Fonda said.

The Eagles—all of them—had just come into the amphitheater and sat in front of Jane Fonda, Cher, Clint Eastwood, Lorraine Chaney, Franny, and Jimmy Carter. The Eagles included Timothy B. Schmidt, Vince Gill, Don Henley, Deacon Frey, Joe Walsh, and sometimes Steuart Smith.

Bob Dylan, Neil Young, and Kris Kristofferson were now warbling on stage "And the Times, They Are A-Changin'."

The Eagles all sat up and said, "Yeah!"

"Which is the drummer?" Clint Eastwood asked.

The Eagles laughed. "It's a mystery," Timothy B. Schmidt said.

"We'll tell you later," Vince Gill said.

"OK, we'll take it to Hollywood," Clint Eastwood said.

"OK, it's me," Don Henley said. "I'm the drummer and vocalist. We're all vocalists plus our guitars and keyboards or bass."

"Great," Lorraine Chaney said. "Like Charlie Watts is the drummer for the Rolling Stones."

Franny loved Bob Dylan and was his best friend. Bob Dylan was her best friend. She also loved as friends, and they loved her as friends, Bruce Springsteen, James Taylor, Micki Jagger and the Rolling Stones, including Charlie Watts, Ron Woods, Keith Richards, and David Crosby. Tiffani also loved the music of the Eagles, including "Hotel California," "Take It Easy," and "Peaceful, Easy Feeling."

Best of all, Franny loved Bob Dylan, and his "Everybody Must Get Stoned," "Ain't Gonna Work On Maggie's Farm No More," "The Times They Are A-Changin'," and "I Wonder If You've Ever Really Really Really Really—Really—Loved A Woman." She actually loved every one of Bob Dylan's over six hundred rock songs, Bruce Springsteen's "Baby, We Were Born To Run," James Taylor's "You've Got A Friend," and Micki Jagger and the Rolling Stone's "Hey—Hey—You—You—Get Offa My Cloud." And tons of other rock songs by Bob Dylan's super-stage legend rocker friends and the super-stage legend rockers she loved as friends, and they, like Bruce Springsteen, James Taylor, Micki Jagger, David Crosby, Cher, and Jane Fonda, and also King Charles and Prince Will, loved Franny as a friend.

At intermission, Jann Wenner, publisher and founder of *Rolling Stone,* was backstage with Bob Dylan.

"Bob Dylan is great!" all the rockers, and Jane Fonda, Bruce, Franny and Cher, Micki Jagger, Charlie Watts, James Taylor, Keith Richards, Ron Woods, David Crosby, producer Daniel Lanau, King Charles, and Prince Will, etc., had said.

"Jane Fonda, what have you been doing?" Lorraine Chaney asked.

"I've been in a movie with Cher. You ought to go to it. It's really good," Jane Fonda said.

"Cher and Jane Fonda, what did you do in the movie?" Clint Eastwood asked.

"Jane Fonda and I were race car drivers on the NASCAR circuit," Cher said. "We both liked the same guy all during most of the movie."

"Was he a race car driver?" Clint Eastwood asked.

"Sure was. We were all top drivers," Cher said.

"I was the best," Jane Fonda said.

"Anyway," Cher said, "At the end of the movie, I feel sympathetic to Jane Fonda's feelings, so I let her and him get together. I fall in love with a horse rancher and the leader of an Apache tribe, Geronimo. So it all was 'happily ever after.'" Cher said.

"We'll take it to Hollywood," Clint Eastwood said. "When does it come out?"

"Soon," Jane Fonda and Cher said.

Intermission was over. Bob Dylan, Neil Young, and Kris Kristofferson were rocking to "I Wonder If You've Ever Really Really Really Really—Really—Loved A Woman."

It was a far-out night.

Bob Dylan introduced "Beat Generation."

We're the Beat Generation
We Never Get Old
We're Not S_____ C_____

We're the Beat Generation
Yeah!"

The rocker and super-stage legend rocker audience of all generations loved it and yelled, "Yeah!" and the rocker yelled-.

The Eagles, James Taylor, Bruce Springsteen, Micki Jagger, Mikey, Charlie Watts, Ron Woods, Keith Richards, David Crosby, Santana, Jane Fonda, Cher, Clint Eastwood, Franny, and Lorraine Chaney were all enthusiastic with joy.

"I wanna sing that "Beat Generation" song with Bob Dylan," Bruce Springsteen said.

"I care—I care about being part of that unbeatable generation," King Charles, who had come in at intermission, said to Bruce Springsteen.

"So Bob Dylan will keep his generation going like he wants to with "Beat Generation," Jann Wenner said. "Like he did with "Everybody Must Get Stoned," "The Times They Are A-Changin'," "Like A Rolling Stone," and "I Wonder If You've Ever Really Really Really Really—Really—Loved A Woman."

"And also with the legalization of marijuana," Bob Dylan told Jann Wenner of *Rolling Stone* when Jann Wenner asked Bob Dylan what he felt about keeping his generation going, which was what Jann W. felt was the major dramatic question for a *Rolling Stone* cover article.

Chapter 4

The Bob Dylan band rocked on.

Bob Dylan had a new stage costume, as did Neil Young and Kris Kristofferson.

The amphitheater manager, Tony, and Earl, the floor staff manager, loved Bob Dylan's music as they did all the stage rockers and super-stage legend rockers.

Tony had amphitheater women to the side backstage, counting the tickets so they would know how many rockers attended.

Earl had directed all the amphitheater guys and chicks of his to their places in the concert arena to direct crowd flow and check tickets and show where certain seats were.

Paul Nedemiere, another amphitheater manager, was down from Los Angeles helping out.

Everybody loved Bob Dylan's concerts.

Mikey, a Nederlander executive, as all amphitheater managers were, had come in from a western state with Nederlander, worldwide entrepreneur of rock concerts.

The California amphitheater was a popular one and filled to capacity, as most Nederlander amphitheaters were because they had super acts.

"And The Times They Are A-Changin'." Bob Dylan rocked on his harmonica. The band around him cavorted on stage with him and rocked to the music.

Cher and Jane Fonda were sitting near the front and had saved places for Tony and Earl, who were going with them to an after-concert party.

Cher and Jane Fonda had met Tony and Earl several concerts ago when they were taking a tour of the amphitheater.

Mikey had a sports section in the back of his super-stage legend rocker and stage rocker magazine called *Nederlander's Rock On.*

The first article featured this introductory paragraph: "Cher, Jane Fonda, and Nederlander executives, Mikey and Franny and Susie, and Bob Dylan and Bruce Springsteen and Micki Jagger and James Taylor love sports, so this sports section on women and men race car drivers has been included in *Nederlander's Rock On.*

Chapter 5

James Taylor was a horse rancher who knew Geronimo. He gave for renumerance horses to Geronimo, one to Jane Fonda, one to Bob Dylan, and one to Bruce Springsteen. James Taylor gave a white pony with a lush mane to Cher since she was Geronimo's girl.

There was a *Life* magazine put out just on Bob Dylan, commemorating his birthday. The whole magazine was about Bob Dylan.

James Taylor, Franny, and Bruce Springsteen love Bob Dylan. Bob Dylan loves Franny, Bruce Springsteen, and James Taylor.

James Taylor was a super-stage legend rocker, like Bob Dylan and Bruce Springsteen, and Micki Jagger.

James Taylor had been in another magazine, *Annual Guitarist*, with a fine double-page picture spread and several pages about James Taylor. It was a cover story with James Taylor's picture on the cover.

Franny had written cover stories too for several magazines, James Taylor reminded her. They included "Industry," "Heavy Duty Trucking," "Video Store," "Orange County Illustrated," and "The Sportswoman."

James Taylor went off in his red car to congratulate Bobbee Dylan on another cool cover and whole magazine for his birthday.

Chapter 6

Franny sat at an ice cream place, working on a perspective drawing of two chairs—a Chippendale chair and a Hepplewhite—and watching for Bob Dylan and Clint Eastwood.

Both had just gotten in from Los Angeles.

Bob Dylan had been in concert last night. Clint Eastwood had just finished producing a Jane Fonda and Cher movie about two women race drivers. Cher wins until Jane Fonda wins at the end. Cher went to an Apache reservation and fell for the leader of the tribe, who owned a horse ranch.

Bob Dylan, realizing that Cher and Jane Fonda liked race car drivers and hot amphitheater rockers, found out the next day about the Lawrence and Topeka races and called Jane Fonda and Cher to invite them out to be with Clint and him and Franny.

Bob Dylan, Franny, and Clint Eastwood loved racing and race cars.

In fact, Bob Dylan got an Indy race car—red and black—and practiced racing on the off days at his local race track.

Clint Eastwood got excited and brought his film men out to cover Bobbee's antics.

Franny and Bobbee sometimes sat in the stands while Franny took notes and wrote for a rocking car magazine. Bob Dylan wrote racing songs.

Cher invited the Apache actor who had been in her race car movie out to be with her, and Jane Fonda got the amphitheater manager,

Tony, who liked to do a motorcycle race in his spare time, to come on the scene.

It was a happening time for Bobbee, Franny, Bruce Springsteen, Clint Eastwood, Jane Fonda, and Cher.

Bobbee Dylan, Bruce Springsteen, Franny, Cher, Jane Fonda, and Clint Eastwood walked through the pits of the race, talking to the other drivers and pit crews.

The leader of the Apache tribe, Geronimo, was off looking at horses he might get with Tony, the amphitheater manager.

Bob Dylan was racing today, and his pit crew, Kris Kristofferson, and Neil Young were getting his car ready.

Jane Fonda and Cher were racing tomorrow.

Bob Dylan and crew went down to his black and red Indy race car.

Cher and Jane Fonda were also racing in this race.

Franny was racing in an SCCA (Sports Car Club of America) race soon.

Bob Dylan climbed in through the window of his car. Kris Kristofferson and Neil Young ran up to encourage the plucky super-stage legend rocker.

Bob Dylan pulled up onto the race track and lined up with the other Indy cars. Bobbee revved his engine.

The race was on.

$$* \quad * \quad *$$

Bob Dylan sped into a tight circle, then vroomed the gas to speed into a straightaway.

Ahead of him, three cars had the lead so far.

Bob Dylan moved ahead, got behind the second car, and let her momentum speed him along.

It was Cher, and she tried to outrace him, but Bob Dylan ducked around her and came out just three lengths behind the super-fast first race car.

Bob Dylan kept on traveling speedily and zoomed around the course.

Jane Fonda came around Bobbee Dylan from the far side and almost crashed into the wall.

Jane Fonda swerved and headed into the way of all the Indy race cars, then righted herself and found her way back into the race, now in fifth place.

After twenty-five turns around the course, Bob Dylan noted the flag that showed the finish line was coming up next time.

The first car was now one and a half car lengths ahead of Bob Dylan.

Kris Kristofferson and Neil Young on guitar flashed to Bob Dylan, rock-singing "You Know You Can."

Bob Dylan stepped on the gas and sped up. Faster and faster. At the finish line, he nosed by the guy who had been first by half-a-car length. Almost a photo finish!

Franny and Jann Wenner, publisher and founder of *Rolling Stone*, were waiting in the "Winners Circle."

The next day, Franny's and Jann Wenner's stories on Bob Dylan—the winner—appeared in four places, with more to come.

Bob Dylan was happy. Bruce Springsteen, Franny, and Jann Wenner were happy. Everyone was happy.

Chapter 7

Bob Dylan took Franny, Tony, and Cher off to view horses at a horse ranch Geronimo wanted to appraise.

Bruce Springsteen and Jane Fonda were racing NASCAR that Saturday.

*   *   *

You Are My Franny-Love
and I Keep You Happy.
—Bob Dylan

*   *   *

Bruce Springsteen took a practice turn around the track. A Black in a two-toned blue patterned hooded sweatshirt, black jeans, and white slip-on canvas shoes viewed Bruce Springsteen over the railing.

Jane Fonda pulled her orange NASCAR car with lots of decals around and vroomed and waved as she went by the Black.

Bruce Springsteen and Jane Fonda were racing today, both in hopes of winning.

Jane Fonda took a lot of risks and was lucky, very.

Bruce Springsteen drove with determination, bravery, and dedication. Both were excellent drivers.

*   *   *

Jane Fonda got the lead early and kept on.

Bruce Springsteen found her groove early and rode behind her, taking her speed along with his.

The other NASCAR cars zoomed behind. Helio Castroneves zoomed ahead.

Bruce had twelve laps to go. He stayed in his comfortable race place behind Jane Fonda, now in second.

At eight laps to go, Bruce made a pit stop. The guys ran out, changed his tires, checked his car out, then signaled to Bruce everything was OK.

Bruce sped up the long lane to the race course.

Bruce took the lead. He didn't notice Helio Castroneves, who was probably in the pits too.

Bruce won the race. Jane Fonda came in second.

*   *   *

"I'm gonna sing for you tonight," Bob Dylan said to Franny.

Jane Fonda, Cher, and Bruce Springsteen came to the after-concert party.

*   *   *

In the next race, Jane Fonda kept noticing in the rearview mirror when Bruce Springsteen rode her tail. Jane Fonda dropped back slower, and Bruce Springsteen had to go around.

Jane Fonda rode Bruce's tail zoom, and Jane Fonda won the race.

*   *   *

At the next concert, Bob Dylan announced to his wildly enthusiastic rocker audience: "My 'Everybody Must Get Stoned' and 'Franny' songs are popular. I put it on my world transmission."

"The 'Beat Generation' spawned kids, and they all loved their parents and all generations after them, and it continued with them," Cher announced at her next concert about Bob Dylan's "Beat Generation."

"Baby, I love Cher and Dick Dale people," Bob Dylan said.

Dick Dale people had been a commune once and now were on a farm in Phoenix with over a hundred people. These included Dick Dale's sixteen sons: Dickie, Ricki, Micki, John, Johnny, Josh, Robert Allison, Christopher, Doug, Clint, Phoenix, Ryan, Alexander, Oliver, Deacon, and Joe.

The Dick Dale people barreled into the race track stands and took seats at several turns and curves in the race course.

Chapter 8

"The Eagles like you," Joe Walsh and Deacon Frey of the Eagles said when they came down to be with Franny at Bob Dylan's request after a Bob Dylan concert.

Neil Young had reminded Franny the Eagles liked her. "And Timothy B. Schmidt of the Eagles liked you when he came down a couple of times first," Neil Young said.

The other Eagles were Don Henley, the drummer, Vince Gill, and sometimes Steuart Smith.

"What did Keith Richards say?" Bob Dylan said.

"He said he wanted to date Jane Fonda, and she might like him," Franny said.

Another Eagle came down in a truck, then another Eagle that day.

"I might like to date Cher. Keith and I can sit in the stands together and watch Jane Fonda and Cher race," Neil Young said to Bob Dylan.

"I'll be racing too and Bruce Springsteen," Bob Dylan said.

"I like to have fun," Bob Dylan said.

"We all do," Mikey said.

Concert Nederlander, who had rock amphitheaters all over the world, came in and sat with Mikey.

"Lots of the Eagles and their friends were down here," Neil Young said.

"I like them all, and so does my father," Concert Nederlander said.

"Baby, I've come up with something that's very important and has wonderfully written all over it with 'Beat Generation,'" Bob Dylan told Franny.

On Thursday, a rocker came in and said to Franny and Bob Dylan, "I love 'Beat Generation,' particularly for all generations, and I love Bob Dylan and Bruce Springsteen and Bob Dylan's band and the Eagles and Neil Young and Kris Kristofferson—all of 'em," he said.

The "Beat Generation" was a rock song Bob Dylan wrote that Bruce Springsteen and the Eagles wanted to sing too.

"Can we sing it?" the Eagles asked Bob Dylan.

"Of course," Bob Dylan said.

Bruce, of course, didn't have to ask. He and Bob Dylan were that close.

*　　*　　*

Theater Nederlander was up in the stands, watching the race with Franny, his son Concert Nederlander, Mikey, and Clint Eastwood.

"My son, Concert Nederlander, loves concerts. That's why he chose concerts to shepherd all over the world," Theater Nederlander said, "and he's good at it if I do say so myself."

Theater Nederlander was a mostly US-nationwide-and-some-world entrepreneur of plays and movies. He was possibly going to work with Clint Eastwood.

"Legalization of marijuana—that's what we all care about," Theater Nederlander said just as the race started.

"Yeah," everyone said.

Bob Dylan had come up earlier before the race and had told Franny, "I like to wear a black T-shirt under a stage outfit." Last night at his concert, Bob Dylan had worn a black T-shirt under a green silk jacket and black stage pants.

Chapter 9

Bob Dylan was reading a *Rolling Stones* magazine when William Shatner came in and sat down with him.

"Hi, William Shatner. What's going on?" Bob Dylan asked.

"I'm thinking of a new TV series—*Bowling Capers*—starring me, William Shatner," he said. "I could run a bowling alley and be a captain on one of the teams. And we could have a national bowling championship match twice a year. What are you doing, Bob Dylan?"

"My band and I are rockin' magnificent concerts," Bob Dylan said. "What will you do in the bowling league?"

Franny came in.

"Oh, just a minute. Hi, Franny. I'm here for you," Bob Dylan said, kissing her. Franny kissed Bob Dylan.

"Franny, here—bring a chair from another table and sit down with me," Bob Dylan said.

Franny did. Bob Dylan and Franny hugged.

"Anyway, I need all the help I can get to develop this series," William Shatner said. "I could have a Ron Dean behind the counter flirting with the ladies and being on my bowling team."

"Sounds good," Bob Dylan said.

"Yeah," Franny said.

"Maybe we can have a Black guy—Charlie—running the snack bar and soft drinks department," William Shatner said.

"Hey, cool," Bob Dylan and Franny said.

William Shatner was wearing cool black tennis shoes with a white check from back to front, medium grey slacks with a hint of black under pattern, and a burgundy T-shirt.

Franny was wearing yellow slacks and a yellow, orange, and purple striped shirt.

Bobbee Dylan, Bruce Springsteen, and Clint Eastwood always planned to come into William Shatner's bowling alley to have fun after their rock music and producing careers and get ideas for more rock songs.

Chapter 10

Queen Elizabeth came to the races and congratulated Bob Dylan for winning, as did Prince Charles and Prince Will.

Queen Elizabeth, in a navy suit and heels and pearl necklace, came to the Indy 500 race to view Bob Dylan's and Prince Charles's race.

With her were sixty Buckingham palace guards.

At the race, Prince Will sat with Queen Elizabeth and the Buckingham palace guards.

Intrepid Bob Dylan and Prince Charles zagged and zigged and scampered over the race strategy inherent in the course.

Queen Elizabeth, used to attending Wimbledon tennis matches, horse races, and a few other important sports events, loved the Indy 500 races.

The forty-nine sports cars zoomed and vroomed through the course—round the track—through the pit stops, and ultimately, intrepid Bob Dylan, concert singer/songwriter extraordinaire, won the Indy 500.

Prince Charles was a close second.

Concert Nederlander was in the race stands, along with Theater Nederlander 2 and Nederlander 3 and Mikey, Nederlander executive.

All of them loved Bob Dylan, Prince Charles, and the races.

In the Winner's Circle, the racing promoter presented Bob Dylan with a gold trophy, a pretty girl kissed him, and news broadcasters interviewed Bob Dylan.

They also ushered in Queen Elizabeth, Prince Charles, the second winner, and Prince Will.

BOB DYLAN, BRUCE SPRINGSTEEN, & ROCK FICTION 25

Queen Elizabeth regally and sincerely congratulated Bob Dylan on his race car win and also congratulated Prince Charles.

Prince Charles and Prince Will hugged Bob Dylan, who hugged them. Jann Wenner of *Rolling Stone* and Franny, as journalists, came into the Winner's Circle.

"I love racing," Bob Dylan told them. "This is a good day for me." Bob Dylan hugged Franny and thanked Queen Elizabeth, Prince Charles, Prince Will, and Jann Wenner.

Micki Jagger, Bruce Springsteen, James Taylor, and David Crosby ran up and got on the TV, radio, newspaper, and magazine news with Bob Dylan and Prince Charles in the racing Winner's Circle.

Clips of Bob Dylan and Prince Charles navigating and zooming through the race course were shown on the 11:00 news.

"Bob Dylan does it again," *Rolling Stones* thundered.

"Nederlander's Rockin' Review" had articles by Mikey and Franny about Bob Dylan, Prince Charles, the race, and Bob Dylan's conquering win amid his concerts.

Queen Elizabeth, Bob Dylan, Franny, Prince Charles, Prince Will, and all the super-stage legend rockers and Buckingham palace guards and race rockers celebrated at a roadhouse Bob Dylan appropriated for the evening.

"Quite an honor to be photographed by Jann Wenner and Franny in the Winner's Circle," Bob Dylan told them later over Cokes at the roadhouse.

It was a rocking evening.

*   *   *

Neil Young looked at Bob Dylan's chicken tenders.

"That looks like enough for two," Neil Young said.

"Have some," Bob Dylan said.

"Thanks, Bob Dylan," Neil Young said.

Will of England came in with Kris Kristofferson.

"Hey, dudes. Get one of these chicken tenders—enough for two," Neil Young said.

Will of England and Kris Kristofferson came over with their own lunch.

"I went to you guys' concert last night, Bob Dylan, Kris Kristofferson, and Neil Young," Will of England said. "You guys were fantastic. I love you and your band, Bob Dylan!"

"Thanks," Bob Dylan, Neil Young, and Kris Kristofferson said.

"Grandmama came to the United States from England to view your concerts and the races," Will of England said. "She sailed over on a luxury liner. She loves boats."

"That's great. We'll have to do a special concert for Queen Elizabeth, won't we, Bob Dylan?" Neil Young said.

"Rockin' right!" Bob Dylan said.

Kris Kristofferson drummed on the table.

*　　*　　*

They were at William Shatner's bowling alley on Gage.

Concert Nederlander and Mikey took a bowling lane about ten lanes from William Shatner's.

Mikey got spares, open frames, and one strike. Nederlander beat Mikey's 172 by ten points.

Chapter 11

Clint Eastwood came down from California with Lorraine Chaney to race with Bob Dylan and Bruce Springsteen.

"Lead us to the NASCAR races," Clint Eastwood said to Bobbee and Bruce.

"Yeah, I want to race!" Lorraine Chaney said.

"You got it," Bob Dylan said.

"We were there when President Dwight Morgan gave a speech in California about decriminalizing marijuana. I love that dude," Clint Eastwood said.

"Yeah, he's a great president," Bob Dylan enthused.

"Well, I just know we're going to get marijuana legalized," Lorraine Chaney said.

Clint Eastwood hugged and kissed her. Lorraine Chaney kissed Clint Eastwood.

With the sign-ups done at the NASCAR races, Clint and Lorraine went off to view the two race cars Bob Dylan and Bruce Springsteen had secured for them.

Lorraine's was purple; Clint's was black with purple, red, and yellow stripes and decals.

"Let's go!" Bob Dylan said enthusiastically. He popped into the passenger seat of Clint Eastwood's, while Bruce Springsteen opened the passenger door of Lorraine Chaney's car.

Bob Dylan viewed the race track zoom by as Clint Eastwood stepped on the gas.

Prince Will waved as they went by the second turn. Prince Will was sitting with the Eagles, Dick Dale and his sixteen sons, Micki Jagger, and James Taylor.

Bruce Springsteen and Lorraine Chaney sped past right after, then Lorraine Chaney zoomed ahead.

Clint Eastwood was a softy, he always said afterward.

"Ha ha! I won. You know I did!" Lorraine Chaney always said.

Bobbee, Bruce, the Eagles, Lorraine Chaney, Clint Eastwood, Dick Dale, and his sixteen sons, and NY and KK all went out for coffee and Cokes at the huge NASCAR race track coffee shop.

Prince Charles, Prince Will, and Queen Elizabeth were already there, with the Buckingham palace guards, discussing racing.

"Bob Dylan, guys, you got time for a little extra racing today?" Prince Charles asked.

"Sure. What's happening?" Bob Dylan said.

"Will and I are planning to race this afternoon," Prince Charles said.

"Yeah, we got new NASCAR cars, and we tried them out yesterday," Prince Will said.

"Far out!" Bob Dylan and Bruce Springsteen said.

"When are you going to do that? I'd like to view that!" Mikey said.

"Yeah," Robert Allison, one of Dick Dale's sixteen sons, said.

"Right after lunch sounds good," Clint Eastwood said. "OK?"

"Sure," Prince Will and Prince Charles said.

"Where's Franny this afternoon?" Clint Eastwood asked Bob Dylan.

"She went over to view the SCCA Race Track with Jane Fonda and Cher. She wanted to surprise me by racing soon," Bob Dylan said. "Jane Fonda and Cher are going to race with her."

"We gotta go view that race, right, Dad?" Prince Will asked.

"Sure thing, Will," Prince Charles said.

Franny, Jane Fonda, and Cher came in.

Bob Dylan and Franny kissed and hugged.

"What's up?" Cher asked.

"We're racing this afternoon," Prince Charles said.

"For a practice," Prince Will said.

"Want us to race with you?" Jane Fonda asked.

"Sure, that'd be cool," Prince Charles said.

"Let's finish here and get down to the course!" Bob Dylan said.

"Yeah," they all said.

Chapter 12

"Baby, I had a wonderful concert (tenth summer concert)," Bob Dylan said.

"Baby, I loved that picture. It's an inspirational picture of Bob Dylan doing anything," Bob Dylan told Franny. Franny had drawn pictures of Bobbee, Neil Young, and Kris Kristofferson, and also of Bobbee and Bruce leaning and reclining on cool motorcycles or riding on motorcycles.

"It's gonna be a good day for you," Prince Charles had said that morning.

"Baby, let's go. I had a marvelous concert last night. Go draw. I'll be coming with the Eagles, Bruce, James Taylor, Micki Jagger, Neil Young, Kris Kristofferson, and be with you soon," Bob Dylan said to Franny.

James Taylor, Neil Young, Micki Jagger, and Bruce Springsteen came by in a red pickup truck with Bob Dylan and Kris Kristofferson.

"That's the best picture you ever did of me," Neil Young said.

"It's cool, cool, cool," Bob Dylan said, "and abstract," he said of the picture of Bobbee and Bruce.

"Yeah, far out!" Bruce Springsteen said.

*   *   *

It was right after the Eagles had come to a Bob Dylan concert that Bob Dylan had asked the intrepid guys to come over to Franny, where she hung out.

Timothy B. Schmidt and Joe Walsh came in first. Timothy Schmidt of the Eagles was wearing a white T-shirt, black open vest, and jeans. Joe Walsh had a red T-shirt and jeans.

Bob Dylan came in with a big art magazine and *Easy Riders* and *Rolling Stone* magazines and sat with Franny.

As Joe Walsh and Timothy B. Schmidt of the Eagles were getting their fast food at the counter, Randy Meisner, one of their friends and a former Eagle, drove by the drive-through in a station wagon with a big white bulldog and the guy's girlfriend sitting beside him.

Deacon Frey strolled in in a red sleeveless T-shirt and black silk stretch slacks with a stripe on each leg. Clint Eastwood came up right after and stood at the counter with Deacon.

"You're with the Eagles, aren't you?" Clint Eastwood asked. "I dig your music. We can take it to Hollywood."

"Great. Come out and do a movie anytime at one of our concerts," Deacon Frey told Clint Eastwood.

Bob Dylan and Bruce Springsteen had black Harleys parked outside. Neil Young and Kris Kristofferson rode up on theirs and parked beside them.

Soon all the Eagles, Bob Dylan, Tiffani and Bruce Springsteen, Clint Eastwood, and the crew were sitting together around a long table.

Neil Young, Bob Dylan, Kris Kristofferson, and Bruce Springsteen were writing a song inspired by Franny, "Fantasy Girl."

She's Our Fantasy Girl
She Writes and Draws Adventures
She Imagines
For Us—Our Fantasy Girl.
—Bob Dylan, Neil Young, Kris Kristofferson, and Bruce Springsteen

Chapter 13

Bob Dylan and Micki Jagger were watching Micki Jagger's film and idly scanning through pictures of football players on the sports pages.

"Movie's good," Bob Dylan said, handing Micki Jagger a big bowl of cheesy popcorn.

"Wait. It gets better," Micki Jagger said.

Neil Young came in with Kris Kristofferson.

Kris Kristofferson, in a long brown T-shirt and black jeans, said hi to Franny, who was drawing all of them on a sketch pad Bob Dylan had given her.

Then Kris Kristofferson said hi to everyone who said hi to him.

Bruce Springsteen came over.

Bob Dylan kissed and hugged Franny.

"We're talking about marijuana legalization," Neil Young said.

"Hope it happens," Kris Kristofferson said.

"It will," Micki Jagger said.

*   *   *

"Legalizing marijuana or decriminalization has been due for a long time," Prince Charles said with respect to Bob Dylan.

"A far-out idea. I love it, as I've always loved it whenever I've found it considered," Bob Dylan said.

"Outstanding!" Prince William agreed.

Queen Elizabeth rang for tea, which was brought immediately with scones and bagels.

*   *   *

During this marijuana-legalization possibility in which smoking recreational doobies was now legal in states in the United States, they all smoked a joint in marijuana-legal Colorado, including Prince Will, Prince Charles, Bob Dylan, Franny, Bruce Springsteen, Micki Jagger, Jane Fonda, and Cher.

Chapter 14

Clint Eastwood and Lorraine Chaney each won a NASCAR race.
Bob Dylan and Bruce Springsteen each won five races.
Prince Charles and Prince Will each won two races.
Jane Fonda and Cher each won four races.
Bob Dylan and Bruce Springsteen were racing today.
Bob Dylan won the next race.

*   *   *

Jane Fonda had been interested when Keith Richards came down and mentioned he was interested in Jane Fonda because she was a race driver.

Jane Fonda, who had studied with a race car driver when she was doing her last movie, joined a race car driving school and got another fantastic race car driver to teach her tactics.

*   *   *

And I Would Not Feel So All Alone
Everybody Must Get Stoned.

Bob Dylan, Neil Young, and Kris Kristofferson rocked out.
The Eagles—all of them—had just come into the amphitheater and sat in front of Jane Fonda, Cher, Clint Eastwood, Lorraine Chaney, and

Jimmy Carter. The Eagles included Timothy B. Schmidt, Don Henley, Joe Walsh, Vince Gill, and Deacon Frey.

Bob Dylan, Kris Kristofferson, Neil Young, and the rest of the band were now warbling on stage "And The Times, They Are A-Changin."

"Beat Generation"

Now Bob Dylan and his band rocked to "Beat Generation."

We're the Beat Generation
We Never Get Old
We're the Beat Generation.

Prince Charles and Prince Will were in the audience, and they and all the other rockers sang with Bob Dylan, Neil Young, Kris Kristofferson, etc.

We're the Beat Generation.

Chapter 15

Prince Charles and Prince Will were waiting with Queen Elizabeth the day Bob Dylan brought Jane Fonda and Cher to meet Queen Elizabeth.

In truth, Prince Charles was happy to meet Jane Fonda and Cher. Probably, even the Queen would like it, Prince Charles felt.

He knew he was not hard to meet, and maybe he had already met them. Prince Charles met so many people in the course of his duties.

"Queen Elizabeth, may I present Jane Fonda and Cher," Bob Dylan said after saying hello to Prince Charles and Prince Will.

Bruce Springsteen had already met Queen Elizabeth and knew Prince Charles and Prince Will from when Bob Dylan had introduced them in California.

Bruce Springsteen was standing among the well-wishers in action at the British party.

"Queen Elizabeth, I'm so happy to meet you," Jane Fonda said, curtseying.

"Happy to meet you, Queen Elizabeth, and I'll dedicate a song to you," Cher said, curtseying also.

"You two are fantastic. I love your movies and songs, Cher and Jane Fonda," Queen Elizabeth said.

"So do I," Prince Charles said.

"Ditto," Prince Will said.

"This calls for a drink," Bob Dylan said.

Prince Charles called an usher by nodding, and the Cokes and drinks were immediately procured.

Queen Elizabeth that evening wore a blue dress with a sparkling tiara and shoes to match the outfit.

*   *   *

"Bob Dylan is always good to me, and I am good to him," Franny told Bruce Springsteen at the party.

Bob Dylan kissed Franny, and Franny kissed Bob Dylan.

Chapter 16

Bowling Capers

William Shatner, Bob Dylan, Franny, Bruce Springsteen, and Clint Eastwood, producer, were sitting around at William Shatner's bowling lanes.

"My ninth concert last night was magnanimous, wonderful!" Bob Dylan said.

"That's wonderful, Bob Dylan!" Franny, Bruce Springsteen, and they all said.

"Thanks," Bob Dylan said.

They all looked at the first script for William Shatner's new TV series.

William Shatner sat at a bowling lane with three teammates—Jane Fonda, Charlie, the Black manager of the bowling alley restaurant and snack bar and soft drink stand, and Ron Dean, the flirtatious guy behind the counter where shoes and bowling balls were checked out.

Two chicks—Tori and Georgia-May, in cool red skirts and navy long-sleeved tops—were warming up on the next lane.

They were waiting on the rest of their team, Gabriel and Wolfgang.

*　　*　　*

Donald Sutherland went into William Shatner's bowling alley.

Donald Sutherland greeted William Shatner at the ball and shoe checkout counter.

"I learned you got this bowling alley," Donald Sutherland said. "Wanna partner?"

"I might," William Shatner said. "Let's go over to the snack bar, get a Coke or coffee and talk about it in my office."

When the partnership was done, Donald Sutherland noticed Franny interviewing Betty, a national bowling champion who had just won her title in the Shatner/Sutherland bowling alley.

Donald Sutherland brought them drinks and sat with them.

"You're good," Donald Sutherland said to Franny when the interview was done for *The Sportswoman*.

"Thanks," Franny said.

"Do you want to do a four-page *Bowling Newsletter* for me?" Donald Sutherland asked.

"Sure, that'd be great," Franny said.

When she was ready, Donald Sutherland and Franny went over to his office and finalized the newsletter.

Bob Dylan came over, fresh from a cool concert yesterday, and they all went bowling.

Chapter 17

Keith Richards came down to the race track to visit Jane Fonda.

"Where's that Jane Fonda?" Keith Richards of the "Rolling Stones" said. "She's a race car driver. I've never dated a race car driver before."

Keith Richards was wearing beige canvas slip-on shoes with a dark brown triangle accent on the side of the instep, black socks, jeans, a light red cool T-shirt, and dark grey hooded sweatshirt.

Inspired by Keith Richards, Neil Young said, "I feel I might date Cher."

Bob Dylan, Bruce Springsteen, Micki Jagger, Prince Charles, and Prince Will came down with Jane Fonda.

"Hey, Keith Richards, what's up?" Jane Fonda asked.

Keith Richards and Jane Fonda got coffee together privately, while Cher came in with Neil Young and some other drivers and sat with Bob Dylan and Bruce Springsteen, etc.

Jane Fonda had been interested when Keith Richards had come down and mentioned he was interested in Jane Fonda because she was a race driver.

Jane Fonda, who had studied with a race car driver when she was doing her last movie, joined a race car driving school and got another fantastic race car driver to teach her driving tactics.

*   *   *

Bob Dylan was adorable. He sat in the stands at the race track, where he was going to meet Franny in a second. Bruce Springsteen was with him.

Bobbee wore a very cool navy shirt, nudged down at the collar by sunglasses, light blue jean shorts, and cool yellow-rimmed and tied navy tennis shoes.

Franny came up the stands to Bobbee and Bruce.

They all had waved.

Down below, the race was getting ready to start.

Jane Fonda and Cher were both racing in an SCCA (Sports Car Club of America) Ladies' Event race.

Vroom, vroom. The cars revved up in the sweet sound of racing motors.

About twenty-five cars were lined up below on the race track.

The cars were stretched out in a long line.

"I see Jane Fonda," Bob Dylan said. "Third from the front."

"And there's Cher, about twelfth back," Bruce Springsteen said.

"Yeah, that's them!" Franny said, waving at them. Cher and Jane Fonda waved back.

Keith Richards and Neil Young spotted Bob Dylan, Franny, and Bruce Springsteen in the stands and came up to join them.

"It's gonna be a good race," Bobbee said. "Cher and Jane Fonda are here. That's who we came to see."

"Us too," Keith Richards said, "I've never dated a racing woman before. I came out to view some action and discover whether Jane Fonda wants to go out dancing or something."

Chapter 18

"Love is important, Franny," Bob Dylan said and hugged Franny. Franny hugged Bob Dylan.

"I care about you, Baby—a lot," Bob Dylan said.

"I love you for your hope," Bob Dylan told his adorable Franny.

"I love you incredibly, Bobbee," Franny told Bob Dylan.

*   *   *

The Eagles came down to visit Franny when Bob Dylan asked them to. The Eagles—Don Henley, the drummer, Vince Gill, Timothy B. Schmidt, Deacon Frey, and Joe Walsh—were at a Bob Dylan concert when Bob Dylan asked them.

Bob Dylan had given Franny the idea for a book as a gift. The idea, Bruce Springsteen said, was an example of Bob Dylan's love for Franny.

I know a lot of rock bands besides the ones I introduce you to, like Boston too," Bob Dylan said, "and Aerosmith. (Bob Dylan had mentioned them several times throughout the years.)

Bob Dylan had already introduced Franny to some of his best friends, like James Taylor, Micki Jagger, Bruce Springsteen, Prince Charles, Prince Will, and David Crosby.

"The Eagles—they were there when you started the book—the Eagles will like it," Bob Dylan said.

The Eagles, like Bob Dylan and Bruce Springsteen, loved being on stage.

When the Eagles performed, they stretched across the stage with Don Henley, drummer and vocalist with his lots of drums and cymbals, across the back. Across the front were guitarists, bass, and keyboards by Timothy B. Schmidt, Vince Gill, Deacon Frey, Joe Walsh, and Steuart Smith.

The Eagles' songs include "Take It Easy," "Hotel California," "Peaceful Easy Feeling," and "Life In The Fast Lane."

Bruce Springsteen, Bob Dylan, Mikey, (Nederlander partner), James Nederlander 1, James Nederlander 2, and N 3 liked to go to Eagles concerts and the super-stage legend rockers, their own, and their friends' concerts, and the Nederlanders—all concerts.

Prince Charles and Prince Will came down from England to see Bob Dylan and Franny.

Susan Farley, artist and college art teacher, and college president Jerry Farley (both from Washburn) also came down.

*   *   *

Jane Fonda, Cher, Bob Dylan, Franny, and Bruce Springsteen met Danica Patrick, the first woman to lead the pack in an Indy 500 race. She came in fourth that day.

"On a much smaller scale, my best friend Franny came in fourth at an SCCA Ladies Event. Her friend Pam was first," Bob Dylan said.

"Ah, the dreams of the drivers who watch us in the Indy 500," Danica Patrick said.

Danica Patrick won that day.

Bob Dylan, Bruce Springsteen, and Cher gave Danica Patrick tickets to their concerts, and Jane Fonda gave Danica Patrick passes to her and Cher's movie about being president and vice president.

Chapter 19

Bob Dylan, Jane Fonda, Bruce Springsteen, and Cher zoomed into the Indy 500 races and began winning—first, Bob Dylan, then Jane Fonda, then Cher, then Bruce. They all took firsts time after time.

"I love watching you grow in talent, Franny," Bob Dylan said as Franny wrote article after article of him and the others winning.

"I love being part of the unbeatable generation," King Charles said.

Prince Will was excited by the races.

Danica Patrick and Helio Castroneves zoomed past and took firsts and seconds.

As they were racing, Ron Woods ran up into the stands with *USA Today*.

"Legalization of marijuana," the headlines read. "States for recreational marijuana and more was happening," the article said.

"One thousand or more motorcycle riders celebrate the legalization of marijuana in states," the article went on and then said, "Motorcycle riders include Bob Dylan, Kris Kristofferson, Neil Young, Bruce Springsteen, Eagles, Cher, Jane Fonda, Nancy Sinatra, David Crosby, Micki Jagger, Ron Woods, Keith Richards, Mikey, Jann Wenner, Nederlander 1, Nederlander 2, and Nederlander 3."

President Joe Biden and his wife, Jill Biden, came down to race in the Indy 500 for a *Saturday Night Live* skit.

Saturday Night Live got interested in President Joe Biden and First Lady Jill Biden winning the Indy 500 for a skit.

SNL created a skit where Jill Biden was an experienced race driver. She was teaching President Joe Biden recreational racing for the Indy 500.

Both wanted to win.

President Joe Biden and Jill Biden met Helio Castroneves, Danica Patrick, and the super-stage legend rocker racers like Bob Dylan and Bruce Springsteen.

President Joe Biden and Jill Biden had fun and came in first and second at the Indy 500.

"President wins, First Lady second at Indy 500," the headlines and TV news declared on SNL.

*   *   *

At the *Saturday Night Live* party that night, Bob Dylan proposed a toast to President Joe Biden and First Lady Jill Biden for winning at racing.

Bob Dylan came over to Franny. Bobbee won many races at the Indy 500 and loved Franny. When he came over through the SNL crowd, Bob Dylan said to Franny, "I know I'm a wonderful man. I have a wonderful girl to be wonderful for."

It was a magical moment.

Bruce Springsteen and President Joe Biden and Bob Dylan led the rockers in singing Bob Dylan's "Beat Generation."

Chapter 1

A few years after sports car racing, Bob Dylan and Bruce Springsteen went mountain climbing with some of their friends.

Jane Fonda and Cher sent word that they were involved in a new movie and couldn't go mountain climbing, but they would try to make it for any parties that might come up.

First, the sports aficionados went to the Olympics.

Bob Dylan and Bruce Springsteen were in the stands at a pairs ice dancing Olympics contest.

Bob Dylan had met Franny much earlier at a couple of big sports events—wrestling, boxing, etc.—after first meeting her at a concert.

Franny was a freelance journalist who worked for a number of magazines.

Franny was up near the front, recording the action by the scorekeeper.

Bob Dylan kept a seat for Franny in case she should come up, which she often did between events.

Bob Dylan and Bruce Springsteen were close friends. Bob Dylan was a gregarious cool guy who smoked marijuana in all the US states where it was legal, like Colorado, California, Alaska, Washington state, Washington DC, Oregon, and other states, and where it wasn't legal, he was always hoping it would be legal soon, and he always did what he could to make it legal.

A cool couple danced out from the United States. They ice skated, twirled, and spun beautifully, dancing in perfect rhythm.

After a long competition, which Bob Dylan, Bruce Springsteen, Franny, and Micki Jagger, who had come back from getting a coke, loved, England finally won.

A gold medal was the highest award possible (the United States eventually got nine), followed by a silver medal (the United States earned eight), and third place was a bronze medal (the United States. got six).

Jimmy Carter and his nephew Paul the artist, came over and sat near Bob Dylan, right in front of him and his group. Jimmy Carter and Paul had met Bob Dylan first at a national skateboarding contest, which they all loved, and then at a concert.

"Individual skating is next," Bob Dylan told Jimmy Carter and Paul.

"Cool," Jimmy Carter said.

The next day, they all watched snowboarding.

This was Paul's favorite Olympic event, except for skateboarding, which he did himself. Jimmy Carter also liked his nephew's favorite events, which included skiing, which they both loved.

"We don't know who the champion will be yet, do we, Paul?" Jimmy Carter asked.

"Not yet, but I love snowboarding. It's really great!" Paul said.

Bob Dylan said, "I like snowboarding too. So do you, right, Bruce Springsteen?"

"That's right, Bob Dylan," Bruce Springsteen said. Bob Dylan liked his friends to know each other.

In the next few days, they were all getting ready to watch an actual snowboarding competition.

In the US Women's Division, the United States received a gold medal in women's snowboard, slopestyle, and a silver in the ladies' big air snowboard. The United States obtained a gold medal in the women's snowboard half-pipe.

"This is really great," CR said to Franny. CR was a Hollywood producer-director directing a film about the 2018 Winter Olympics.

"I wonder how the US men will do in skiing," Bob Dylan said.

"I bet they do great," Franny said.

The US men earned a gold medal for half-pipe skiing.

All the other winners so far had been for the United States too.

In the competitions, the United States won the silver medal in the men's big air snowboard.

Bob Dylan, Franny, Bruce Springsteen, Micki Jagger, Jimmy Carter, and Paul were all particularly interested in the one-thousand-meter short crack speed skating contest. The United States won silver.

The group went over to women's skiing.

"Hurry!" Franny said, running over. "The US women are doing great in skiing!" The United States got two silver medals for women's half-pipe freestyle skiing and ladies' alpine combined skiing.

Bruce Springsteen, Micki Jagger, Bob Dylan, and Franny went over to watch the curling teams perform afterward, then they all did.

In curling, the team shoves a large weight down a large patch of ice to try to make it go as far as it will go.

Bruce Springsteen, Micki Jagger, Bob Dylan, Jimmy Carter, and Paul were excited to note the US men's curling team won a gold medal, as was Franny.

On another day, the United States got the silver medal for women's bobsled.

"That was great!" Franny said.

"Baby, we were born to run!" Bruce Springsteen said, quoting one of his favorite rock songs, as he liked to do.

Bob Dylan hugged Franny. "Did you get notes on all that?"

"Sure did, Bobbee!" Franny said.

Chapter 2

They had just watched Lindsey Vonn get a bronze medal for women's downhill skiing.

Now they were all sitting around a cafe at the Olympics.

"Soon, we're going to have even more fun too," Bobbee said.

"Oh, what are you going to do?" Jimmy Carter asked.

"We're going mountain climbing to reach the top of Mt. Whitney called Denali by the Indians in Alaska, the highest peak in the United States," Bobbee said.

"Well, that's certainly a commendable goal," Jimmy Carter said.

"Yeah, Mt. Whitney is also the third highest peak in the world," Bruce Springsteen said. "Bob Dylan has already talked me and James Taylor and Micki Jagger into going."

"Franny is going with him to get the experience of mountain climbing first-hand. She might stop at the halfway way station on the mountain or go part-way up and come back down and wait for the team to come back from the summit."

"Bonnie's going too," James Taylor added. "She's the photographer we met with her family at the Olympics. Her husband and two teen girls are going back to California so the girls can go back to school. He's an auto mechanic with his own business."

"Nederlander's coming too," Bob Dylan said. "We joined him at the Olympics."

"I might go too with Paul. We can stop at the halfway way station on the way up the mountain to do research for 'Reaching the Summit' paintings," Jimmy Carter said.

"Sounds good, Uncle Jimmy," Paul said.

*   *   *

"How many people have climbed Mt. McKinley?" James Taylor asked.

"Just a handful in the first sixty years of the 1900s," Bobbee said. "Then, from 1960 to 1999, about 22,300 tried to climb to the top. Over a thousand strived to do it in 1989. Then, starting in 1992, at least 1,000 per year."

"That's a lot," Bruce Springsteen said.

"Many of the mountaineers depended on professional guides because they had almost no high altitude experience," Bobbee said.

"Most of the climbers since 1970 have ascended the West Buttress."

CR loved his mountaineering experience more because of Lorraine and because he was producing/directing a movie.

Bob Dylan had gotten a deep friendship started with Franny, his best friend, who he had known for a long time.

She planned to go on the mountain climbing trip part way with Bobbee and the team, then go back to the halfway way station with Mikey and Susie to wait till they came back so she could interview Bobbee and the team about reaching the summit and what they did.

*   *   *

The Talkeetna air taxi service went every day from the hotel to the halfway way station, where most climbers started from if the weather was good.

They dropped off mountaineers at Mikey's and Susie's halfway way station.

"The base camp established here is managed by a camp manager who remains in radio contact with pilots and National Park Service rangers," Paul, the lead guide, explained to Bonnie, Bobbee, Franny, CR, and the other climbers who had gotten off the three air taxiplanes at the way station.

"After we've gotten the tents and igloos set up, we'll go in the way station and eat our last home-cooked meal," Paul continued.

"I'm going to sure enjoy that before we climb the mountain," Bob Dylan said.

"That'll be great, Bobbee," Bruce Springsteen said.

"I sure am glad I hired John to bring us up lots more food and another cookstove," Bobbee said.

"This'll be a great trip up, Bobbee," Paul, the guide, said.

The mountaineers devoted a good two hours at the halfway way station with energy rations like steak and candy bars.

"This all is pretty good, hey?" Micki Jagger asked.

"Sure is, Micki Jagger," Bonnie said.

Jimmy Carter and his nephew Paul, the artist, took photos of the climbers for the paintings they planned to do for *Reaching the Top of Mt. McKinley.*

*   *   *

Paul, the lead guide, and the other guides, Mikey, Susie, and George, led the group through the mountain's ice and snow up to another camp at 7,500 feet. They carried food and fuel for the little cookstoves, sleeping bags, and tents up five miles, yet only three hundred vertical feet.

Chapter 3

On the mountain climbing trip, Bob Dylan trekked with his favorite friends, Bruce Springsteen, James Taylor, and Micki Jagger. The three were among the Bard's closest friends, as was Paul McCartney. Franny was Bob Dylan's best friend.

CR, the film director and producer, had been encouraged to go with them by Bobbee, James, and Bruce.

Their guides were George, Nedermiere, and Paul. Mikey and Susie, who ran the halfway way station at the halfway up point, but the beginning point of most climbs on Mt. McKinley, guided if needed, and if they were, the guards on Mt. McKinley would take over running the way station for them.

The halfway way station was where most climbers pitched their base camp.

Mt. McKinley, at 20,320 feet above sea level, was the third-highest peak in the world and the highest in the United States. It was in Alaska.

* * *

Bobbee climbed up the first leg of the Mt. McKinley snow-covered cliffs from the air taxi to the halfway way station.

Right behind him were Franny, James Taylor, and Paul, the guide, followed closely by Bonnie. Then, Micki Jagger, Bruce Springsteen, and CR and Nedermiere.

"I see a good spot for our base camp," Bob Dylan said, "I marked it with four wands. We can put up a large tent and two igloo tunnels."

"Do you have your tents and all your gear yet?" Susie asked. She was their waitress as well as assistant manager of the halfway way station.

"Yep, got it all," Paul said.

Mikey, the manager, brought them steaks and baked potatoes. Susie brought them coffee lattes.

The Rolling Stones were on the radio with "Satisfaction."

Franny, Bobbee's friend and a journalist, was interviewing them all about how they felt getting ready to climb Mt. McKinley.

"Find an outline or theme for the film," CR, the producer/director, wrote in his notes.

Chapter 4

Bob Dylan was watching Susie and CR playing cards and talking in one of the smaller tents while Bruce Springsteen, Mikey, Micki Jagger, and Paul were also playing cards.

Susie and Mikey were going as guides part way up with Franny, Jimmy Carter, and Paul, who wanted to experience the feel of mountain climbing without trekking all the way to the summit.

Franny, the journalist, Jimmy Carter, now a painter, and his nephew Paul wanted to record the experience or paint a portrait of those making it to the summit.

Susie and Mikey would guide them down when they wanted to go, leaving Paul, the head guide, Nedermeire, and George to guide the others on the way up to the top of Mt. McKinley.

Franny, Paul, the nephew, and Jimmy Carter would then stay at the halfway way station to wait for Bobbee Dylan and the others.

"What other things have you done, CR?" Susie asked, laying an ace on his ten of spades.

"Well, I have my private pilot's license, and I fly airplanes, and I'm a producer/director in Hollywood," CR said.

"CR, Mikey spends five to six months of the year as an amphitheater manager in California, and he really likes working here and also working for concerts. I'm working with Mikey next year, even though I was born here in Alaska. I could probably get Mikey to get you to work as one of the amphitheater managers or assistant managers.

"Mikey is a top amphitheater manager. They also have a floor staff manager and assistant manager, which I am, who oversee the concert crew, a maintenance manager, a backstage manager who deals with the concert rockers, and other managers and assistant managers who work in the office, dealing with Mikey as he does videos of band hopefuls who want to be opening acts, or scheduling the stars, etc.," Susie said.

"I might like that, Susie," CR said. "I might also like to film it and do a movie on it like I am on this mountain climb. Jane Fonda is looking for a movie to do with Cher and Kris Kristofferson and her boyfriend, Patrick."

"Let me know," Susie said.

CR won the hand.

"Maybe you can fly me and Franny and Bruce up to California with you, Susie, and Mikey, CR," Bob Dylan said.

"Maybe I can get Jim to take us in his plane," CR said.

"Hey, that'd be great, CR," Bobbee and Franny said.

Chapter 5

After setting up tents and igloos, the team ate another mountain meal.

Bobbee and the others ate one or two tuna fish sandwiches, sausage, bagels, and cream cheese and drank coffee.

Jimmy Carter and Paul, his nephew, the artist, were having fun climbing Mt. McKinley part-way.

"I've never been to the summit," Jimmy Carter said. "Paul and I just might go with you."

"That'd be great if Susie also guides us to the top," CR said. "I like her company."

At the next camp, as they set up the tents, Paul, the guide, said, "Probably tomorrow, we'll have to cut ice steps into the glacier to go up."

"I'm for that. I'll maybe help you, Paul!" Bobbee said.

"Okay. We'll see if Mikey, Nedermiere, Susie, and I need help. Thanks a lot, Bobbee," Paul said.

For food for breakfast the next day, they each had four slices of French toast with jelly. Some could only eat two or three slices.

"The high altitude takes away some people's appetite," Paul the guide said. "Try to eat as much as you can."

"Mountain climbers go through lots of calories," Susie said.

"The view of the Alaska Range is excellent—look!" Micki Jagger said.

"Yeah, you're right!" James Taylor and Bob Dylan said.

By the end of the day, they had cut lots of steps into the ice to make the climbing easier.

Chapter 6

At the next camp, at 9,500 feet, the mountain climbers had to make two trips to carry their supplies up. They rode down to their earlier camp to get the rest of the supplies on plastic sleds.

On the way up to the eleven-thousand-foot camp, Paul and Mikey cut large steps into the ice to help the team up.

It snowed that night as they set up their tents and ice igloos.

"Do you want to go back tomorrow?" Bobbee asked Franny, Jimmy Carter, and Paul.

"We'll see how the weather is," Jimmy Carter said. "Unless Franny goes to the summit, then we'll probably go. There's only two guides extra to take us."

"I'd kind of like to make it to the summit," Paul, the nephew, said. "But it's up to you."

The next day, they stayed in camp because of the snow, and the day after that, they all made it to camp at eleven thousand feet.

Bobbee set down his backpack and sat on it. Franny sat beside him in the tent.

"Tonight, we can zip our sleeping bags together and probably stay warmer," Bobbee said to Franny. "If you want to."

"Well, Lorraine and CR have been doing it most of the way up, so I guess so," Franny said.

They hugged and drank the hot cocoa Susie brought everyone. Paul and Mikey were making dinner on the cookstove.

The next camp—at 13,500 feet—they finally reached at nine in the evening through light snow.

The next day, they used crampons and ice axes to get to their 16,400-foot camp.

Crampons were special spiked footgear that was strapped on or clamped to the bottom of climbing shoes to give traction on ice or hard snow.

Chapter 7

As Bobbee, Bruce, Micki Jagger, James Taylor, and George and Nedermiere, the two guides, were helping Paul, the head guide, cut steps, Paul said, "This is the Muldrow Glacier. As you can see, the glacier has two steep walls. The right one goes to the North Peak of Mt. McKinley. The left wall eventually summits at our destination, the South Peak."

The camp was set up on Muldrow Glacier eventually, after cutting many ice steps and after equipment and supplies were ferried up.

At this time, CR, Paul, the guide, Bobbee, Bruce, James Taylor, and Nedermiere went out the next day in an advance party to mark out a safe and secure run.

Venna and Micki Jagger, Bonnie, the photographer, and the others waited at the last camp until the advance crew got back. When they did, Jimmy Carter and his nephew, Paul, and Bobbee's friend, Franny, who were only going part-way, would then go back with guides Mikey and Susie to the halfway way station to wait for the others.

*   *   *

The temperatures went from extremely cold in the night and mornings to very hot at noon and the afternoons.

Just beyond the 11,500-foot camp, the Muldrow Glacier came to a steep end.

Above them rose a great icefall that divided the upper and lower glaciers. The mountaineers would have to go up the Northeast Ridge leading to the upper bowl.

The advance team went back to camp and told the others. Bonnie took one last series of photographs of everyone. Then Franny, Jimmy Carter, Paul, the nephew, Mikey, and Susie went back down to the halfway way station to wait for the summit climbers.

The summit adventurers faced a hard and careful three weeks getting up the ridge.

The way up through the jumbled mass of ice blocks and rocks was hampered by a few days of white-out.

At the white-out, they had to stay camped while they still could.

While they were playing cards and talking, Paul, the lead guide, said to Bobbee, Bruce, James Taylor, Nedermiere, and Bonnie, who he was playing cards with, "You know, I'd really like to have a girlfriend. Someone who would naturally fit into my leading trips to the summit all the time."

George, another guide, said, "You might want to go to more of Melissa's parties. She's the manager of the hotel at the base of Mt. McKinley, and she gives lots of parties after mountain trips. You might meet lots of people there. I'm a silk screener too, and I live at the base of the mountain."

"So do I," Paul said.

Chapter 8

Micki Jagger liked Venna, his girl, who did exciting things on her own—skiing, boating, and now mountain climbing (as the team did).

Venna wore turtlenecks, bright-colored sweaters, jeans, and hiking boots.

Paul played chess with Bob Dylan. Bob Dylan said, "Paul, when you get a girl, I hope she gives you sympathy, and I hope you give her sympathy."

"I'm sure that'll happen," Paul said. "I'm going to Melissa's party after this trip."

"Great, that'll be terrific," George said, watching Paul and Bobbee play chess. "You know, Paul, you might even like Melissa, who manages the hotel at the base of Mt. McKinley and gives the parties. I think you'd like her. She owns a sailboat she keeps in Newport Beach and lives on it when she's there."

"Thanks, George," Paul said. "If I like her. I've never liked a girl who lives on a sailboat."

Ellen, a photographer, who was coming down the mountain after reaching the summit, told Paul, Bobbee, Bruce, and the rest of the team that she would be back, and she might meet them some time at one of Melissa's parties.

Bobbee was glad his friends were starting to find girlfriends on the mountain. He always liked his friends to care about each other.

Bobbee was also glad Franny would be waiting for him at the halfway way station.

Bob Dylan wanted to be interviewed by Franny.

"I really like the oyster stew," Ellen said.

Bobbee, James Taylor, Bruce Springsteen, and Paul made sure they had plenty that night. Ellen and her team stayed with them.

CR filmed the group for his Hollywood film.

The two groups moved off, up or down, from camp, taking advantage of the good weather.

First, they had lunch.

Ellen, a good photographer, Bonnie, and CR had fun taking pictures.

"I'll be sure to get Melissa to keep the film and pictures at the hotel for you after I get them developed," Ellen promised.

"I'll pick them up from her and give them to everybody," Paul promised.

Bonnie, Bobbee, Paul, CR, Venna, Micki Jagger, and James Taylor were most anxious to get to the summit of Mt. McKinley.

Chapter 9

CR was directing a film on climbing Mt. McKinley with Bobbee, Bruce, and Paul's team when he got back to Hollywood.

Susie really liked anyone who did great things (like the team of mountaineers).

CR would recreate the mountain scenes back in Hollywood.

Susie took lots of pictures before she and Mikey guided the part-time climbers back to the way station. She was Mikey's girlfriend.

CR took lots of films.

CR was particularly glad Susie and Bonnie were there. He had told Susie and the team what he was doing.

While Ellen was there, she had taken some great photographs of CR, Susie, Bobbee, Paul, and the team playing cards in the big tent and in the landscapes.

Bonnie and CR had taken lots of photos of Paul, Bruce, Bobbee, and Franny, when she was there, and Jimmy Carter and Paul, his nephew, the same, and whatever else CR had wanted, including the scenery.

Susie drew and, while she was there, occasionally drew CR and the others.

She made one drawing of Bobbee, Bruce, CR, and Paul, the guide, in front of the Alaska landscape.

Bobbee wished for the team to reach the summit and then hike back down to the halfway way station so he could see Franny.

Still, he wished to see and spend time at Mt. McKinley's summit, which was the goal of the mountaineers.

Venna said to Micki Jagger and Bob Dylan, "This is so much fun and so exciting. I don't know if I'll ever have this much fun again."

She looked sad.

Micki Jagger said, "We haven't even got to the top yet. Venna, why don't we come back to Mt. McKinley again and get married at the summit? Bob Dylan and Paul, you'd come back with us, wouldn't you?"

The guys said, "Sure."

"OK, that'd be great! I love it," Venna said. "Thanks, Micki Jagger!"

Chapter 10

The way was now clear for the group to reach the summit of the ridge.

They established a camp at the pass that gave way to the upper glacier—the Grand Basin.

"Let's put the fifteen-thousand-foot campsite here," Paul said.

"OK," Bobbee said and dropped the pack that held the tent.

"Still above on the left is the South Peak, our goal for the top," James Taylor said.

"Yeah, this climb up is not really a technical challenge. It's a test of strength, good judgment, and endurance," Bobbee said.

"Yeah," Micki Jagger said.

"This is Parker Pass," James Taylor said.

The group went up while adjusting to their tolerance of increased cold and decreased oxygen.

"The nighttime temperature here is ten to twenty-one degrees below zero," Paul said.

When they set up camp, the mountaineers stayed warm enough, thinking of their heavy caribou and sheep skins to sleep in beneath down quilts and camel's hair blankets and sleeping bags.

"It's hard to get used to thin air," Paul said. "Packing forty pounds is very hard at a high level, even exhausting."

"You said it," Bonnie said. "I'm glad we just got here and can rest."

"Yeah, we've had to stop for needed rest stops every dozen or so steps," Bruce Springsteen said.

"Let's set up high camp here. This looks like a good spot," James Taylor said.

"I think you're right. This is about eighteen thousand feet," Paul, the guide, said, consulting a barometer.

"Great. That puts us less than 2,500 feet from the top! We can do that in a day," Bobbee said.

"Yeah, we've got two weeks of food and fuel, and if we had to, we could stretch that out to three weeks maybe, so in case we get stuck in camp, we can still make it to the summit and back," James Taylor said.

The next day, the team left high camp at 7:00 a.m., taking only enough food for lunch and dinner and instruments for summit measurements like a barometer.

"This is perfect," Bruce said.

The weather stayed clear and calm, good for a climb to the top.

"Are you monitoring for frostbite, everyone?" George, the guide, asked.

"Yeah, I checked. Everyone has plenty of gloves, mittens, and socks," Paul, the guide, said.

"So far, so good, right?" George said.

"Yeah, we're great!" everyone said.

"I'm a gentle guy, so I'm looking forward to meeting girls at the hotel party after we get to the summit," Paul said.

"I'm not thinking about the party yet. I'm looking forward to that just for fun, but what I most really want right now is the summit— getting to the top!" James Taylor said.

"Yeah, let's do it!" Bobbee Dylan said.

The mountaineering team kept going on their way up and finally stopped for a lunch break.

"This hot coffee is great. Thanks, Nedermiere and George," CR said.

"Yeah, this warmth cheers me up and makes me sure we'll make it to the top," Bruce said.

"I feel great about making the trip today," Bobbee said.

"We all do!" Micki Jagger said.

"Are we all ready to go on?" Paul asked.

"Sure," Bruce said, getting up to pack his backpack and handing Venna hers, which Micki Jagger helped her with.

"Let's go," Bobbee said.

The group of mountainers started again on their way up.

Chapter 11

At 2:30 p.m., James said, "Wow. Is that the summit just a little ways ahead?"

"Yep," Bobbee said. "It's just a few yards away!"

Bob Dylan hurried forward. "I'm the first on the top! Hurry up, guys. We made it!"

"Let's get this small tent set up, so we can take some instrument readings," Paul, the lead guide, said.

"I've got the aneroid and mercury barometers," Bobbee said.

"And I've got two kinds of thermometers," Bruce said.

"Someone take a summit photo of me for my husband and kids," Bonnie said.

"I'll do it," CR said. "Stand over there by that great view of that other mountain."

"That's the 17,400-foot Mount Foraker, and it looks good from our 20,300-foot summit of Mt. McKinley," Paul said.

"Let's all get in a group photo and then get the photographer in the group and someone else to take the picture," George said.

"I'll do it!" Bonnie said. "I'd like a 'photo by Bonnie' in a magazine if I could get one, and a group photo with me too, and my single picture of just me for my husband and kids."

"That Mt. Foraker is known as Sultan, Denali's wife," Paul said.

"Also, look to the east and south at that view of an infinite range of mountains, which goes all the way out in a curve of the whole Alaska range from Mt. McKinley to the sea," Bobbee said.

"Wow, that's great. You sure know a lot," CR said, filming it. "Let's get a picture of Paul and you and Bonnie and that view."

They all, plus Bruce, George, Micki Jagger, and Venna stood posing for the scenic view.

Then Bobbee took a picture of just Paul and CR.

Chapter 12

Carolynne Kim had come to the halfway way station to wait for James Taylor, Bruce Springsteen, and Bobbee Dylan, with Franny (waiting for Bobbee and everyone), Jimmy Carter, and Paul (waiting for everyone to come back so they could begin painting their summit portraits).

While at the halfway way station, Mikey looked out the door.

"There's a group coming about a half mile away," Mikey told Susie, the two Park Rangers helping them, Carolynne, Jimmy Carter, and Paul, the nephew.

"I wonder who it is," one of the Park Rangers said.

"Two of them look like chicks," Mikey said. "Probably Venna and Bonnie and Bobbee and the group we're waiting for."

"Hope so," the other Park Ranger said. "We have a full house in the guest rooms of those waiting for Paul's big group to come back and the others waiting to house them when they do."

"I'll be glad to interview them about the mountain climbing when they get here," Franny said.

"We'll do portraits of the climbers, right, Paul?" Jimmy Carter said.

"Sure," Paul said.

Jimmy and Paul took their sketch pads outside to watch the mountaineers come down the mountain.

Mikey and Susie went out to greet them. The others waited inside to surprise them.

Chapter 13

Alaska had legal marijuana, like some other states like Colorado and California, so, at the hotel, the tourists and mountain climbers were toking on joints.

Mikey had brought them to his table where Bobbee, Franny, and Susie were.

He and Susie had come back to the hotel at the base of Mt. McKinley from the halfway way station with Paul and Bobbee's group.

Franny was interviewing the mountainers while Bonnie took pictures.

"We remained on the summit as long as we could because we realized that being there was a once-in-a-lifetime achievement," Bobbee said.

"After a couple of hours at the summit, we began going down. We had planted a flag with our names and 'We were here' on the top of the mountain. Most of the climbers also left mementos planted or buried in the snow. We reached the eighteen-thousand-foot camp at 6:00 p.m., ending our long summit day," Paul, the guide, said.

"The next day," Micki Jagger said, "We left camp at 9:30 a.m. We entered and left the Grand Basin and then began the most difficult part of the descent. It was the Northeast Ridge."

"Almost two-and-a-half feet of snow had fallen since we had last been there," Bruce Springsteen said.

"Yeah," said James Taylor. "The steps we had carved were covered up with snow and ice, so we had to shovel out the old steps or, in more than a few areas, make new steps."

"We got to the Upper Muldrow camp at 9:30 p.m. after twelve hours of journeying and resumed our descent the next morning," Bonnie said.

"We were tied together on two ropes," Bruce Springsteen said.

Bobbee Dylan continued, "The team very carefully went down the densely creviced glacier, which now had a much unlike face than it had when we traversed it on the way up."

"We made camp to rest up before returning to our descent to the halfway way station. I'm glad we made it to the summit and back without any misadventures," CR said.

"Yeah," Micki Jagger and Venna said.

Chapter 14

At the hotel at Melissa's party, local and national journalists were waiting to interview the mountaineers in Bob Dylan's and Paul's party who had climbed to the summit.

Micki Jagger and Venna danced. Paul and Melissa danced.

When they came back to their table, the journalists were interviewing Bob Dylan.

"Yeah, we're going back and climbing the mountain again, and this time some of us are going to get married at the top," Bobbee said. "Micki Jagger and Venna, and maybe Paul—ask Paul."

"Are you going to get married on the top of the mountain," one of the journalists asked Paul.

"Maybe," Paul said. "I'm starting to date Melissa, who manages this hotel and who has the parties here. I'm going to guide the others up, and Mikey, another guide, and I are studying so we can marry people. By the time we go, I'm going to see if Melissa wants to marry me."

"Why did you decide to get married?" the journalist asked Micki Jagger and Venna.

"I love her, and she's exciting," Micki Jagger said.

"Well, I do lots of things," Venna said. "Plus, I love Micki Jagger, and he asked me."

"What do you do?" the journalists asked Venna.

"Like I said, I do lots of things," Venna said. "So I selected the states where recreational marijuana is legal and went skiing in Colorado, and I have a sailboat in Newport Beach, California, so I go sailing in

California, and now mountain climbing in Alaska with Micki Jagger, who I met at the Olympics."

"And now," Venna said, "Micki Jagger asked me to marry him while we were climbing the mountain, and I said yes. We're going to the summit again when everyone else does, probably in another month or so."

"That's great," a cool journalist said. He then interviewed Bob Dylan, Bruce Springsteen, James Taylor, and the other mountaineers. Last, he interviewed the cool Jimmy Carter and his nephew Paul.

"I have marijuana upstairs in my room. Do you wanna go later?" Micki Jagger asked Venna, Bobbee, Franny, Paul and Melissa, Bruce, James Taylor, Carolynne Kim, and Kate.

"Sure," they all said.

Micki Jagger danced with Venna and was intrigued with his exciting girl, who was intrigued with him.

All the mountaineers were intrigued by each other.

Jimmy Carter, Paul, the nephew, who had been sketching, and CR, who had been filming, came over to join and party with them.

"Like a Rolling Stone" played on the radio.

The next day, newspapers in Alaska and across the United States on the front page reported, "Mountaineers Who Made the Summit Going Back to Get Married on the Top of Mt. McKinley."

The TV news reported the same.

The party at the hotel went on. Rockers loved several-day parties.

Chapter 15

About two months later, a group of mountaineers gathered at the halfway way station for the marriage climb to the summit.

Venna and Micki Jagger, and Paul and Melissa were all getting married at the summit.

Both Mikey and Paul, guides, had taken the course for marrying people and were now like the captains of ships, who also married people.

A lot of the people on the first trip up the mountain with them were also going on this one. This was Melissa's first trip to the summit.

As they stopped for lunch on the first day up, Bobbee Dylan and Franny sat together.

Franny said, "Bobbee, I would like to be a fiction writer as well as a journalist."

Bobbee said, "You know what kind of fiction I like, Franny? I like the kind where only good things happen."

"I do too!" Franny said. "I always read the good stuff and hurry over the part that's otherwise."

"If you write fiction with good stuff in it, I'll help you," Bobbee said. "I'll encourage you to find a publisher."

"Wow. Great. Thanks, Bobbee," Franny said.

They finished lunch and started climbing the mountain again with the others.

Susie was climbing Mt. McKinley with them this time, so she could view the marriages. She was Mikey's girlfriend.

The next day, they stayed in camp because of the snow, and the day after that, they all made it to 11,000 feet.

While at camp, Bobbee set his backpack down and sat next to Franny.

"Tonight, we can zip our sleeping bags together and probably stay warmer," Bobbee said to Franny. "If you want to."

"Sure," Franny said.

They hugged and drank the hot cocoa Susie brought everyone while Paul and George were making dinner on the little cookstove.

At the next camp—13,500 feet—they finally reached at nine in the evening through light snow.

The next day, they used crampons and ice axes to get to their 16,400-foot camp.

*　　*　　*

They passed a group who were on their way down, led by a tall Black brother in a grey parka and hood and black slacks.

"CR, who do you want to marry?" Bruce asked as they were on the way up to the summit to get two couples married.

"Oh, maybe Lorraine," CR said. "We've been friends for years. Or maybe Jane Fonda."

Jann Wenner, publisher and editor of *Rolling Stone* came up with another group, then joined their group.

Franny said, "I should interview you too, Jann Wenner. I'm writing a book about getting married on the summit of Mt. McKinley, or just climbing the mountain."

"Sounds great," Jann Wenner said. "Here, come on with me. Get your tape recorder out and talk to me."

Bob Dylan came over and talked to them.

Bruce Springsteen and CR came over too.

Jann Wenner noted it all for the *Rolling Stone* article he was doing.

"Park Services called me," a guide said, coming up and bringing Paul, the lead guide, over.

"They said Prince Will just called. He wants to climb the mountain with Bob Dylan. Prince Will will be at the party to talk about it after we get back."

"OK," Bob Dylan said.

"OK," Paul said. "Royalty—Prince Will—on the mountain, super-stage legend rockers, like Bob Dylan and Bruce Springsteen and James Taylor and Micki Jagger, and two marriages!"

*   *   *

"This climbing adventure is good," Venna said to Micki Jagger.

"Yeah. Sure is, love," Micki Jagger said. "This is the highest mountain in North America and passes by over a dozen glacial rivers."

They had just gone by Kahiltna Glacier Base Camp on the West Buttress Route.

"I heard more than 80 percent of mountaineers use the West Buttress Route now," Venna said.

"Yeah, this Denali, as the Alaska natives call Mt. McKinley, is fantastic," Micki Jagger said. "By the way, Denali means 'the high one.'"

Bobbee and Franny came up with Paul, Melissa, CR, Lorraine, Jann Wenner, and Bruce.

"The view is fantastic," Lorraine said.

"Sure is," Micki Jagger said. "Look over there."

"Fantastic," Paul, Melissa, and Bobbee said.

"How high is this mountain again?" Jann Wenner (*Rolling Stone*) asked.

"Oh, 20,320 feet," Bobbee said.

"Mt. McKinley's climate (halfway to the summit), a little higher, equals the North Pole," Paul said.

"I saw when I was flying on the bush pilot services that Denali is only a half-hour plane ride from Talkeetna, a small town about 120 miles from Anchorage," Jann Wenner said. "The mountain is super accessible."

"That's right," Micki Jagger said.

"Once we get above Karstens Ridge on the Muldrow Glacier Route, we'll have done the hardest part of the climbing," Paul said.

"That's good to know," CR said. "I hope we get there pretty soon."

George came up.

"However," George said, "beyond Parker Pass, the climb upward has a lot of decreased oxygen and increased cold."

"Which we already know from having been up once before," Venna said.

"The thin air starts at altitudes above fifteen thousand feet," Paul said.

"We'll set up a series of camps while crossing the Grand Basin," he continued. "Then we'll make high camp at about eighteen thousand feet."

"The weather is good," Bobbee said.

"Yeah, sure is," Venna said.

They continued climbing on.

Chapter 16

On the day they reached the summit, they were still five hundred feet away from the top of Mt. McKinley.

It was a clear day.

Micki Jagger hugged Venna and pulled her close to him.

"This is it, baby," he said.

"I love you, Micki Jagger," Venna said.

They kissed.

James Taylor took their picture.

Bob Dylan hugged Franny, who hugged Bobbee. James Taylor and Bruce Springsteen took their picture.

Paul came up, hugging Melissa, and James Taylor and Bruce Springsteen took their picture.

George, the guide and silk screener, sketched quick pictures of them on the mountain for a silk screen T-shirt.

"Come on, guys," Mikey and Susie called, leading at the head of the group.

Bonnie had come, leaving her auto mechanic husband and two teenagers in California, having been talked into it by CR, Bobbee, and Franny.

Bonnie and CR filmed and took pictures.

Lorraine, CR's friend, went to the summit with them this time.

At the top, Paul, CR, and Bonnie picked the most scenic view to hold the weddings in front of.

"I say right here," Paul said. "Here, we have a curving sweep of two mountain ranges behind us all the way out to the sea."

"We agree," CR and Bonnie said. Bobbee, Micki Jagger, and Venna nodded.

Mikey planted a flag, "Marriage at the Summit," to be prominent in front of some of the pictures.

Nedermiere, Mikey, and George set up a CD player set to rock out with "I Wonder if You've Ever Really Really Really Really—Really—Loved a Woman" by Bob Dylan, songs from Bruce Springsteen's "Tunnel of Love," romantic songs from Eric Clapton, and "Hey, Hey, You, You, Get Offa My Cloud" from the Rolling Stones.

Mikey stood ready at a rock he had picked out.

Bonnie, CR, James Taylor, Bobbee, and several others stood ready to take their picture.

Paul kissed Melissa. Melissa kissed him.

Mikey went through the marriage ceremony, the vows which Paul and Melissa had written themselves and spoken caringly, and the rings.

Then he said, "You may kiss the bride."

Photos were taken, and everyone at the summit came forward to congratulate the couple.

Paul and Melissa had been very gussied up in white furry hooded parkas and red mittens.

"You can put these on over your parka hoods," Bonnie had said to Venna and Melissa, handing out veils.

Mikey was ready to perform the ceremony.

Micki Jagger and Venna were next to be married on the mountain's summit.

"I'm ready," Bonnie said.

"So am I," CR said.

"So am I," Mikey said. "Why don't you guys stand right here in front of this magnificent view?"

"I've got the ring on a gold chain till we get to the hotel to Paul and Melissa's party," Micki Jagger said.

"Oh, that's so sweet," Venna said.

Mikey began the ceremony and in the middle, said, "Each of you can hand the ring to your mate."

Micki Jagger gave Venna her ring on a gold chain, and then Venna gave back to him another ring, which Bobbee had quietly put on a gold chain at the halfway way station.

"I now pronounce you man and wife," Mikey said.

The small group ran up and hugged the newly married couple.

Micki Jagger and Venna were very excited at the ceremony and hugged Mikey and every one after they kissed. Micki Jagger cavorted and danced a love dance to Venna, which they all joined in.

Once again, the team of mountaineers ran up to hug and congratulate them.

Micki Jagger, Venna, Paul, and Melissa cavorted around while CR filmed them and all the mountaineers.

"The weather still looks good," Paul, the guide, said.

"Yeah!" George, the guide, said. "Let's hurry, though."

Jimmy Carter and his nephew, Paul, had come all the way up to the summit this time. They were sketching.

Venna and Micki Jagger got one last wedding picture at the summit, standing in front of Mikey, who married them, with the view in the background.

All the wedding couples—Paul and Melissa and Micki Jagger and Venna—got one last hug.

Bonnie, CR, and James took pictures and filmed the two couples.

CR filmed them all together and as couples in front of the spectacular view one last time for the film on mountain climbing he was producing and directing.

Bruce Springsteen, James Taylor, and Carolynne Kim Taylor hugged Micki Jagger, Venna, Paul, and Melissa one last time.

"Congratulations!" Bruce, James Taylor, and all the rest of the team said.

Understanding that almost never could they enjoy such a fabulous view, the climbers stayed at the summit for as long as they could.

But finally, after a little over an hour, they left.

They started off down the mountain to high camp.

"The way down after the summit is a lot of times the hardest part," Paul said. "Let's all be especially careful!"

"OK, Paul!" the team said.

CR continued filming.

*　　*　　*

They reached the high camp (eighteen thousand feet) at about 5:00 p.m. after two hours of descending.

They were tired yet filled with happiness and excitement.

They left high camp the next day at 9:30 a.m. and departed from the Grand Basin.

They left a record of their ascent and two marriages at the summit of the Grand Basin.

Next was the Northeast Ridge after the Grand Basin.

It was the hardest part of the way down.

A lot of snow had come, wiping out the steps they'd cut, so they had to shovel out old stairs or make new ones.

The team got to the Upper Muldrow camp at 9:30 p.m. after twelve hours of going down the mountain. They started down again the next day.

Tied together on three ropes, the mountaineers went down the heavily crevassed glacier.

The group devoted a day to relax before going on with their return journey.

They were very happy because no mishaps happened.

Chapter 17

At Melissa's party at the hotel at the base of Mt. McKinley, Paul and Melissa started it about a half hour after the summit wedding team flew in the air taxis from the halfway way station.

Jimmy Carter, Paul, his nephew, and George, the silk screener and guide, had their working sketches of the weddings on the summit practically done, ready to be transferred to the final canvas or silk screen product.

Melissa was tall, like Paul, and wore colorful sweaters and dark or light slacks. She also wore tiny jangling earrings and lots of bracelets.

Paul wore a light blue sweater and Gentleman's Quarterly slacks.

"Would you like a drink, Melissa?" Paul asked.

"Yes, Paul. Thank you," Melissa said.

"What would you like?" he asked.

"I guess I'll just have a beer for now. I'm so happy about being married to you—and on the summit too!"

Paul kissed his bride. "And I, my sweet."

Paul brought back a beer and one for himself.

A waitress brought them grilled cheese sandwiches. They sat at a table.

"Would you like to dance?" Paul said.

"I sure would. I love to dance!" Melissa said.

On the dance floor, they danced near Bobbee and Franny, CR and Lorraine, and James Taylor and Carolynne Kim.

CR, Bobbee, Paul, and James Taylor brought their chairs, tables, and drinks over by Paul and Melissa.

Micki Jagger and Venna came to join them.

Several people—guys and chicks—came over.

"What did you wear at the wedding?" one girl asked Venna and Melissa.

"Micki Jagger wore a purple parka he brought just for the wedding," Venna said.

"Venna and I both wore veils over our parka hoods," Melissa said. "Bonnie had them in her gear."

"CR filmed it for a movie he's making. Right, CR," Bobbee said.

"I want to direct a film about mountain climbing, with Bobbee and Bruce, and the weddings at the summit, and some of the other climbers in it," CR said.

Prince Will of England came in and joined them.

"Hey, guys," Will said.

"Hey, what's happening?" they all said.

"I'm coming back next month to climb to the summit," Will said.

"We saw all the publicity on Mt. McKinley, and you guys and I want to do it with you again, OK?"

"Sure, that'd be great!" Bobbee said. "Right, Micki Jagger and Bruce?"

"Sure, of course!" they said.

At the mountain party, Bobbee and Franny are now talking with everyone, including James Taylor, James Taylor's wife Carolynne Kim, and his sister, Kate, and Bruce Springsteen.

Neil Young and Kris Kristofferson came to the mountain party with Jane Fonda and Cher.

A gentleman came over to ask Kate, James's sister, to dance with him. She did.

Bobbee Dylan, Micki Jagger, James Taylor, Bruce Springsteen, Paul, the lead guide, and Prince Will were interviewed as mountaineers and as remarkable people. They were photographed by the Alaska News, the NY Times and other national newspapers, and three TV news stations.

Everyone was very happy.

The gentleman who had danced with Kate kept coming back. Kate was happy.

Two guys from *Time* and *Newsweek* came in.

The next day, the front page of the *Alaska News* read, "2 Couples Married On Summit of Mt. McKinley," and "Most Mountaineers at Fabulous Mountain Party are Remarkable."

The other newspapers did the same, and also the TV news.

Chapter 18

Lorraine and CR were first down to breakfast the day after the party.

It was 9:00 a.m. CR and Lorraine were both used to getting up early from being on the mountain.

"When are you going to the concert amphitheater in California?" CR asked Susie.

"Mikey and I are going soon to get things set up so we can start work June 1," Susie said.

"Then I'll go back to Hollywood and my directing and film editing about the same time," CR said. "And back here for Prince Will's climb."

"That's just three to four weeks away," Susie said.

"That'll give me time to edit snow and mountain photos of everyone for reference," CR said.

They didn't wait for the others, feeling they might be sleeping in.

Just as they were about to leave, Bobbee, Franny, and Bruce appeared, so they stayed and had coffee while the others had breakfast.

They all went on one of the daily air taxis to the halfway way station, which was also the base camp for dozens climbing up or down the mountain.

Susie and Bobbee took pictures of CR filming and Jimmy Carter and his nephew, Paul, by the igloos and tents in the base camp.

Mikey joined them, leaving two National Park Service rangers inside.

The many others at base camp got in some of the pictures for CR's reference for the film.

"Let's go in and have brunch," Mikey said after quite a while. "The air taxi back leaves in about an hour. Prince Will should be already there in the cafe, shouldn't he?"

"OK, yeah," Bobbee said.

"I'll be glad to see the hotel again," Franny said.

Back at the hotel, Prince Will signaled to the park rangers, and they brought over a coffee latte and bagels with sour cream for everyone.

"Hi, guys," Prince Will said. "Thought you might like to warm up."

"Thanks, Prince Will," Franny said.

They took the air taxi back, and the view was spectacular.

They had dinner with Micki Jagger, Venna, Melissa, Paul, and Bruce Springsteen at the hotel.

Franny said to Bobbee, "I interviewed Melissa and Paul about the party and their lives on the mountain in guiding or hosting and hostessing parties, and about each other. First, I interviewed Micki Jagger and Venna. I already did us last night."

"Don't forget to do Prince Will about this party and trek up the mountain soon," Bobbee said.

"I'll do it tonight," Franny said.

Just then, Prince Will came over and joined the group.

"How are you doing, Franny?" Prince Will said after they greeted the group.

"Just getting ready to interview you, if it's OK," Franny said.

"Sure," Prince Will said.

"That's great!" Franny said, writing quickly.

"Thank you," she said to Prince William at the end.

"How are you doing on everything?" Prince Will asked.

"Cool," Franny said. "I have reams of notes. My stories should be great."

"That's cool, baby," Bobbee said, hugging her as she hugged him.

The party went on.

*   *   *

Franny had met Will of England when Bob Dylan had asked him to come to meet her.

The first year, Franny and Prince Will enjoyed art, Prince Will of England's recollections of England, Scotland, Ireland, and friendship with and between them and Bob Dylan.

Chapter 19

Prince Will had the Skype video so those in England, like Queen Elizabeth, could see the climb up Mt. McKinley (Denali).

The mountain climbing jaunt in Alaska to Denali (Mt. McKinley's) summit was considered delightful and exciting.

Prince Will and Bob Dylan would be joined by the two couples who had gotten married on the summit and CR and others who had climbed with them.

The press on TV and in the newspapers had gotten Prince Will interested in going.

Kris Kristofferson was being urged to go with them by everyone, so he was going to go.

So, in July, Prince Will and Bob Dylan converged with others to the summit to make their ascent to the summit of Mt. McKinley.

With Prince Will came seven Buckingham Palace guards, Micki Jagger, Bob Dylan, and Bruce Springsteen.

Also with them was CR from Hollywood, who was making a movie of all the climbs, his friend Lorraine, guides from the National Park Ranger Service, Jimmy Carter and his nephew, Paul, who were painting the climb and summit experience, Bonnie, the photographer, and CR's film men.

CR hauled out his producer/director's notebook at the halfway way station.

"Now, we want a shot of the air taxiplanes, and one good one of the one Prince Will is in and then a whole sequence of them climbing out of the plane and walking up to the halfway way station," CR said.

"This'll be fun," Mikey said, drinking his latte.

"Also, the five Buckingham Palace guards who come along with Prince Will and the super-stage legend rock people they're bringing," CR said.

"You mean Bob Dylan, Micki Jagger, James Taylor, and Bruce Springsteen?" Mikey asked.

"That's right," CR said. "Get them all coming in the door of the halfway way station and greeting Mikey and Susie."

"Don't forget, Franny and maybe Venna, Paul, Melissa, and some others will be with them climbing the 20,300-foot West face of the Denali mountain in Alaska," Susie added.

"OK," CR said, "And then we have the five best guides on the mountain going to lead the way up. That's Paul, George, Mikey, Susie, and Nedermiere. George is also a silk screener who's based at the hotel. He does a lot of 'I Scaled the Mountain' or 'I Made It to the Summit of Mt. McKinley' T-shirts and sweatshirts.

James Taylor and his wife, Carolynne Kim, and sister, Kate, burst through the door of the way station.

"Hey, guys!" James Taylor said.

"Welcome," Mikey said. "Where are you coming from?"

"We're just coming from the base camp," James Taylor said. "We came up yesterday. I want to go up with Prince Will and Bob Dylan and Micki Jagger and Bruce Springsteen, if there's any chance of it?"

"There is," Mikey said.

"Have some coffee latte and maybe bagels and sour cream," Susie said. "This is CR, a producer and director from Hollywood who's doing a film on the summit and climbing and Prince Will and the weddings at the top."

"That's great! Hi, CR," James Taylor said. "Bring over some coffee and bagels and sour cream, OK?"

Chapter 20

Prince Will, Duke of Cambridge, looked down from the plane that was taking him to the halfway way station.

Will of England had the National Park Service at Mt. McKinley wire ahead to Mikey so he would know they were coming.

Will wanted to surprise Bob Dylan and climb Mt. McKinley with him.

Will was warmly dressed for the weather, and he had all his gear together.

"The view is gorgeous," Will said as he saw the Alaska Mountain Range below.

They landed close to the halfway way station.

The base camp of tents and igloos was beside it.

Will climbed carefully out.

Five Buckingham Palace guards came with Prince Will, loaded down with gear and sleds.

They all took off for the way station.

"Won't Bob Dylan be surprised?" Prince Will asked, chuckling.

They strode through the door, and Bob Dylan looked up.

"Bro!"

Will of England said, "We knew you'd be surprised. I'm going to climb with you."

"Great," Bob Dylan said.

Bob Dylan and Franny moved over to let Will in the booth with the mountain view. The Buckingham Palace guards took another booth.

Bob Dylan, Franny, Bonnie, and CR's film guy took pictures of Prince Will, then everyone.

Mikey and Susie hurried off to bring them lunch and a coffee latte.

Chapter 21

CR had his notebook out.

Micki Jagger asked, "Mikey, what's the first thing we're going to do when we start climbing the mountain?"

The mountain climbing team had gotten up at about 7:00 a.m., and they were already in the cafe.

The seven Buckingham Palace guards had slept in two rooms with lots of bunk beds.

A Forest Park ranger, G. Jagger, was going along with the guides Paul, George, Nedermiere, Mikey, and Susie.

G. Jagger's siblings—Elizabeth, James, Brad, Wolfgang, Gabriel, Tori, Georgia-May, Jade, Jasmine, Kim, Karis, Liv Tyler, and Lucas— would be at the halfway way station to see him off.

Breakfast was coming.

"Well," Mikey said, "We put on all our gear, pick up our packs, and start walking up the mountain towards the glacier you can see in the distance."

"First, we have a good breakfast," Susie said.

G. Jagger and Susie brought fried or scrambled eggs, toast or bagels, sour cream, bacon, and pancakes.

Bob Dylan, Prince Will, and the rest posed for a picture for CR's film guy, Earl, and sketches for Jimmy Carter and nephew, Paul, and Bonnie.

Micki Jagger, Venna, Bob Dylan, Franny, Prince Will, Bruce Springsteen, and James Taylor posed for more pictures. Jimmy Carter and Paul posed with Bob Dylan, Prince Will, and the other super-stage legend rockers and mountaineers.

Jimmy Carter and nephew, Paul, took exacting sketches of the two teams, emphasizing Prince Will, Bob Dylan, Micki Jagger, Bruce Springsteen, and James Taylor.

Mikey passed around legal Alaska marijuana after breakfast as they finished their coffee or coffee latte.

"Don't get stoned on the mountain," G. Jagger said.

"We won't. We're not even taking joints with us," Paul, the lead guide, said.

"Good. Sounds great," G. Jagger said.

As they left the way station to start the climb, the Buckingham Palace guards pulled a sled with supplies.

"The mountain and the glacier in the distance look challenging," Prince Will said.

"You got it, Prince Will," Bob Dylan said.

Chapter 22

The team—Prince Will, the Buckingham Palace guards, Bob Dylan, Micki Jagger, James Taylor, Bruce Springsteen, etc.—were traversing up Mt. McKinley and stopped for lunch at a spot with lots of big stones to sit on.

They were below the eleven-thousand-foot camp they were going to tonight.

Franny was interviewing them with her tape recorder.

Bobbee was very happy with Franny and the climb and Franny interviewing.

Bob Dylan, Micki Jagger, James Taylor, and Bruce Springsteen, as super-stage legend rockers, posed for a photograph for Bonnie and CR.

Paul, George, Nedermeire, Mikey, and Susie, the guides, brought over lunch and coffee or cocoa to everyone.

Prince Will picked coffee. So did Bob Dylan and Micki Jagger.

Mikey, Susie, Venna, Melissa, Paul, Bonnie picked cocoa.

Lunch was tuna sandwiches, warm beef stew, and bagels with sour cream.

"George, you should do some silk screening of this," Paul, the lead guide, said.

George agreed and took some pictures while he was eating. CR told his film guy to also get some pictures.

Micki Jagger, Venna, Paul, and Melissa sat and enjoyed the view.

"Ever since Bradford Washburn, a great and ever-present mountaineer who loved the West Buttress Route, and his wife, Barbara, had climbed the mountain on their honeymoon, several other couples had done the same, especially since the eighties and beyond," Bob Dylan said.

"However, Barbara Washburn, the first of hundreds of women to climb Mt. McKinley, was earlier," Bobbee continued.

Prince Will, James Taylor, Venna, Micki Jagger, Paul, and Melissa discussed this while they were eating.

Bobbee and Franny joined in. Franny loved being a journalist, and Bobbee loved being with her and on the mountain.

They all packed up and resumed climbing.

Chapter 23

Bob Dylan built an igloo at the 13,500-foot camp in Denali.

Bruce Springsteen helped Bob Dylan build the igloo, as did Micki Jagger, James Taylor, and Paul the guide.

Paul and Melissa enjoyed their trip.

They had before then climbed up and around the massive ice lands, which separated the lower and upper glaciers.

It had taken the team days to get up the ridge on the way to the summit. The ridge was a chaotic mass of rocks and ice slabs.

Now, they were in a big tent while Bob Dylan and some of the guys built the igloo.

Franny, Venna, Susie, Mikey, Will, Nedermiere, and George sipped coffee.

Later, Paul and Bobbee played chess.

Paul and Bobbee were both rather good at chess.

It was a good game.

"Aha, checkmate," Bobbee said.

Paul studied the chessboard for a half hour and got out of the checkmate.

Three moves for him later, Paul had almost won the game. At the last possibility, Bobbee won.

"Good game," Bobbee said.

"Tomorrow, if the weather is good like the reports say, we might be able to make it to Karstens Ridge above the snow and ice-chaotic ridge on the Muldrow Glacier," Mikey, the guide, said. "Isn't that right, Paul?"

Paul, the lead guide, said, "It's a good possibility."

The way up the ridge was slow.

"The mornings and nights have been extremely cold," Prince Will said to Bob Dylan, Franny, and Micki Jagger.

"We'll make it," Bob Dylan said. "We're a hardy group."

"This is the hardest part of the route," one of the Buckingham Palace guards said.

"Hopefully, we'll be OK," Mikey said. "But we're always glad of backup."

Prince Will said, "The youngest to climb Mt. McKinley was ten. That might be a little early for George and Charlotte and Louie."

"Let's just get us up first," Mikey said.

"Good idea," Susie said.

They walked carefully along the ridge on the way up the mountain's summit.

Bonnie stopped at long intervals to take pictures.

Every time Bonnie took pictures, CR and his film man did too.

"Let's take a break," Bob Dylan said at one of these stops.

"Good idea," Micki Jagger said. "Bring out the coffee."

Chapter 24

As they were going up the Muldrow Glacier, Prince Will said to Bob Dylan, "You know, maybe we can take Prince George and Princess Charlotte and Prince Louis when they're fifteen. Prince George will be seventeen when Princess Charlotte's fifteen, and twenty when Prince Louis is fifteen."

"That'd be fine, Prince Will. Maybe combine Princess Charlotte's and Prince Louis's trip," Bob Dylan said.

"We'll see when they get older, OK?" Prince Will said.

"Sure, Prince Will," Bruce Springsteen said.

They continued climbing the mountain.

* * *

Meanwhile, down at the halfway way station, Lorraine Chaney was waiting for CR.

Jimmy Carter and his nephew, Paul, had been there for a day before the team went up, having a great time drawing pictures of the mountain scenery, inside and outside the station, and the air taxiplanes coming and going. Then Jimmy Carter and Paul made the climb with the mountaineers.

Now, the others were all waiting for Prince Will, Bobbee, Franny, Micki Jagger, Venna, Bruce, Bonnie, Paul, Melissa, and the team to come back, hopefully from the summit.

"This storm won't stop CR," Lorraine Chaney said. "Once he gets going, he can do anything."

"The weather report said no storm today, and so far, it's been clear," Venna said. "I wonder how they're doing."

"Oh, probably pretty soon they'll be getting here," Paul, the artist, said. "Maybe the day after tomorrow, maybe later, but soon."

"I've been thinking of some of us flying to California and sailing down to the Panama Canal and back up the Atlantic Ocean, and then back around to the Pacific in my boat," Lorraine Chaney said.

"Annie Smith Peck climbed mountains," Lorraine added. "A scholar studying her wrote this book *A Woman's Place is at the Top*. She climbed several mountains and lectured."

"A woman's place at McKinley is also at the summit, like getting married to Micki Jagger or Paul or climbing," Jimmy Carter said.

"CR's going to do a film on that," Lorraine said.

"A super-stage legend rocker or a guy's place is at the top too," Paul said.

*   *   *

Earlier, in England, Prince Will read the mountain climbing book Franny and Bob Dylan had sent him.

"Grandmama," Prince Will had said to Queen Elizabeth, "I could climb Mt. McKinley with Bob Dylan and Franny in Alaska. It's 22,300 feet and the third tallest mountain in the world, and the largest in the U.S. Also, four people—two couples—just got married there at the summit. Some didn't have much mountain climbing experience. They just had experienced guides."

"That's a cool idea, Will," Queen Elizabeth had said.

"Maybe Bob Dylan will write songs about it," Prince Will said.

CR heard about this and wanted to go and put it in the film he was making about mountain climbing.

Soon, Micki Jagger and Bruce Springsteen had decided to go too, plus several Buckingham Palace guards.

Chapter 25

Bob Dylan climbed up to Prince Will.

They were still on the Muldrow Glacier, the hardest part for the mountaineering team.

Prince Will and Bob Dylan were still enjoying the mountain climb.

"Good thing they warned us this was the hardest part of the trek," Bob Dylan said.

"Yeah, the other climbers have been here twice or even once recently," Prince Will said, trudging over a snow ridge.

"Will of England," Bob Dylan said, "Remember how you got a year with me in the US for your eighteenth birthday?"

"Yeah, that was sure a lot of fun, Bob Dylan," Prince Will said. "I sure did have a lot of fun with you and meeting all your friends.

"Those friends last forever. And I have gone to the US again a lot since then," Prince Will said.

"I really liked having you stay with me, Will of England," Bob Dylan said.

Micki Jagger, Venna, Franny, Paul, Melissa, Bruce Springsteen, Susie, and Mikey came up.

They started a snowball fight.

Paul, Micki Jagger, Bob Dylan, and Will of England laughed as their snowballs hit the mountaineer rockers.

Micki Jagger, Venna, Paul, Melissa, Franny, Nedermeire, Bonnie, George, Mikey, and Susie pelted them back.

Bruce Springsteen ran up and pelted Bob Dylan with a big snowball.

Bob Dylan and Will of England laughed and sat on a big mountain rock when Paul, the guide, called "Lunch!"

They all enthusiastically joined in.

Chapter 26

Bob Dylan and James Taylor rested in sleeping bags at the back of the big cook tents while most of the rest of the mountain climbers were playing at two chessboards, a checkerboard, and cards in the second tent.

James Taylor said to Bob Dylan, "It sure is great we're going to be at the summit in a couple of days with Prince Will and you and the other mountaineers we're going with, like Bruce Springsteen."

"Yeah, that's really far out, James. Prince Will is really excited about going to the top of Mt. McKinley," Bob Dylan said.

Prince Will was one of the pairs playing chess. Paul, the guide, Melissa, Micki Jagger, and Venna were the other two, while Bonnie and Mikey played checkers.

"So Prince Will is excited," James Taylor said.

Mikey brought them coffee and sat down with them on a rolled-up sleeping bag.

Nedermiere and Susie came over.

"Hey, that coffee looks good, Mikey," Prince Will said.

"Here, have some. Hold out your mugs," Mikey said. He poured the last of the coffee into Prince Will's and CR's two coffee cups.

CR's mug said, "I climbed Denali."

Prince Will's said. "To the top and back of Denali!"

Bonnie came over to film them and everyone and to join in the conversation.

"I'm going to send these to the *Saturday Evening Post*," Bonnie said.

"Let me get one of you taking the pictures, OK?" CR said.

The night went on.

Prince Will, Paul, the guide, and Micki Jagger won the chess games.

"I'll get you next time," CR said.

Bob Dylan, James Taylor, Micki Jagger, and Bruce Springsteen posed while CR filmed the super-stage legend rockers and then Prince Will, Franny, Venna, Paul, and Melissa with the group.

Chapter 27

"We're going beyond Parker Pass today, and we're almost to the top. This is almost the last of the series of camps we're making before the summit," Prince Will said to Bob Dylan as they drank coffee with Bruce Springsteen.

"Yes, we're crossing the Grand Basin today, and then we're camping tonight at eighteen thousand feet, right, Paul?" Melissa said as she woke up.

"Don't forget to eat a good breakfast," Paul, the head guide, and new husband of Melissa, said.

Mikey and Susie brought trays of coffee, bagels, cream cheese, and sausage over to Prince Will, James Taylor, Bob Dylan, Bruce Springsteen, Micki Jagger, and everyone.

"Thanks, guys," Prince Will said. "This climbing a mountain really is great, right, Franny and Bob Dylan and Micki Jagger, and Venna?"

"Yeah, Will," Bruce Springsteen said, taking more coffee, cream cheese, and bagels for him and Bob Dylan from Mikey.

Four of the seven Buckingham Palace guards crowded into the tent.

"We've got everything packed up for you, Prince Will, except for the last of your things here," one said. "What with the thin air making everything harder to pack, we wanted to do it for you."

"Thanks, guys," Prince Will said.

Bob Dylan, Franny, Bruce Springsteen, Micki Jagger, Venna, Paul, and Melissa had their sleeping bags off in a corner.

Bob Dylan, used to getting up early, had gotten up first, and they were all awake.

Bonnie and CR came over, photographed, and filmed them as they drank their coffee and finished the last of their sausages, bagels, and cream cheese.

CR grabbed an extra bagel and coffee and handed one to Bonnie and Lorraine, and they sat with him.

Outside, the Buckingham Palace guards and park ranger G. Jagger, and the guides, including Paul, George, Mikey, Nedermiere, and Susie, packed up their two tents and rolled them up for carrying.

Micki, Venna, Paul, Melissa, Bobbee, and Franny led the way with Will of England, Mikey, Nedermiere, Susie, and the Buckingham Palace guards.

A storm came up midday, forcing them to pitch their tents and build an igloo.

Bob Dylan, Bruce, and Paul, the guide, were particularly good at cutting the snow and stacking it up into an igloo.

"Safety to all us mountaineers is important," George said. "We still have plenty of rations, so we can rest here a day or two."

The next day, the storm ended, and the team trekked off again.

Above the eighteen-thousand-foot camp, about nineteen thousand feet, the last of their series of camps while crossing the Grand Basin, came. Everyone was excited.

"Tomorrow, the summit!" Prince Will and Bob Dylan said.

"Right on!" Susie, Franny, Venna, and Bonnie said.

They hugged.

Prince Will was extremely excited.

The temperature outside the tent was below ten degrees Fahrenheit, but everyone was warm inside.

CR went over to see how some of the Buckingham Palace guards were doing in their tent and had his film guy film them as they lay on sleeping bags, played cards, munched on bagels and cream cheese, and drank coffee.

Chapter 28

On the day they reached the summit, Prince Will, Bob Dylan, Franny, Micki Jagger, Venna, James Taylor, Paul, the guide, Bruce Springsteen, and everyone left their packs at the last camp and continued on with only food for lunch and dinner and instruments, like barometers and thermometers.

The mountaineers ascended the final eight-hundred-foot-high ice and snow ridge to get to the summit ridge.

The summit ridge was completely snow-covered.

Prince Will and Bob Dylan viewed the magnificent scenery.

CR and his film guy filmed them, and then Prince Will, Bob Dylan, Micki Jagger, James Taylor, and Bruce Springsteen.

"It was a magnificent accomplishment," Prince Will said. Bob Dylan, Franny, Bruce Springsteen, James Taylor, and Micki Jagger agreed.

Prince Will, Bob Dylan, and the mountaineers planted several flags at the top.

One flag included everyone's picture and the date.

The day was calm and beautiful, clear, the view absolutely beautiful, with the Alaska Mountain Range to the sea.

"Prince Will and Bob Dylan and Franny, and Micki Jagger and Venna, Paul and Melissa, James Taylor, and Bruce Springsteen were here," Prince Will and Bob Dylan and Micki Jagger and Bruce left on their flag.

"We came back with Prince Will and the super-stage legend rockers and the wedding couple people." This flag was signed by Bobbee, Franny, Bruce, Paul, Melissa, Micki Jagger, Venna, Bonnie, and CR.

"We were here with Prince Will and everyone at the top." This flag was signed by Bob Dylan, Franny, Micki Jagger, Bruce Springsteen, James Taylor, Jimmy Carter, and nephew, Paul, Mikey, Susie, Paul, Venna, Melissa, George, Nedermiere, and the Buckingham Palace guards.

Paul, the guide, George, Mikey, and Susie took instrument readings at the top from the barometers and thermometers.

CR and his film guy filmed the mountaineers playing in the snow.

*   *   *

Bonnie, Bob Dylan, Franny, Bruce Springsteen, CR, Micki Jagger, and Prince Will admired the curving sweep of the two mountain ranges behind them, flowing all the way out to the sea.

Prince Will secured a final flag that said, "Prince Will was here. So was Bob Dylan, James Taylor, Micki Jagger, Bruce Springsteen, and a lot of mountaineers." A picture was included.

"The view of Mt. Foraker looks good from our scenic point on the top of Mt. McKinley," Micki Jagger said.

"And to the east and south. I love the infinite range of mountains in a curve to the sea," Mikey said.

"Yeah," Venna and Susie said.

The Buckingham Palace guards stood with the other mountaineers, the married couples, Prince Will, Bob Dylan, Franny, and Bruce Springsteen, as Bonnie and CR's film men recorded photos.

Bob Dylan, Franny, James Taylor, Bruce Springsteen, and Prince Will cavorted in several special photos and film moments.

At the summit, Bob Dylan, Bruce Springsteen, and James Taylor rocked to Bob Dylan's "I Wonder If You've Ever Really Really Really Really—Really—Loved A Woman."

Bob Dylan and the other super-stage legend rockers rock sang this as the wedding couples Micki Jagger and Venna and Paul and Melissa, and Mikey recreated the marriages at the top of Mt. McKinley.

Jimmy Carter and Paul sketched the scene.

CR took a filmed photo series of Prince Will, Bobbee Dylan, Franny, Bruce Springsteen, and James Taylor in front of the mountaineers while Micki Jagger, Venna, Paul, and Melissa danced off to the side.

Jimmy Carter and his nephew, Paul, would later paint masterpieces of Prince Will, Bob Dylan, Franny, Bruce Springsteen, James Taylor, Micki Jagger, and the mountaineers.

These mountaineers included Mikey, Kris Kristofferson, CR, Bonnie, Venna, the other guides besides Mikey, Susie, Nedermiere, Paul, George, park ranger G. Jagger, and the seven Buckingham Palace guards.

Prince Will skyped it all to Grandmama—Queen Elizabeth.

Then, back at the hotel, they continued at the party.

Bob Dylan and Bruce Springsteen rocked on with James Taylor.

And I Would Not Feel So All Alone
—Everybody Must Get Stoned.
—Bob Dylan

Baby, We Were Born To Run.
—Bruce Springsteen

At the party, Cher and Jane Fonda came in to party with Bob Dylan, Bruce Springsteen, Prince Will, Kris Kristofferson, Neil Young, and everyone. They were all buddies, and they joined in the fun.

The mountaineers danced all night and stayed up till after breakfast.

Round Here—
We Stay Up Very Very Late.
—Bruce Springsteen

Come In
Through My Window.
—Bob Dylan

3) Sailing

Part 1

Chapter 1

"I love the freedom of sailing," Bob Dylan said to King Charles.
"You got it," King Charles said.

*   *   *

I Don't Care What They Do
I Don't Care What They Say
What Do They Know
About True Love Anyway?
Come In Through My Window

Bob Dylan sang to Franny.
"I love little feelings—a sigh—like that," Bobbee Dylan said.
They kissed and hugged—Bobbee and Franny.
They were sailing on the Pacific Ocean—Captain Bobbee and First
Mate Franny.
Dolphins—seven of them—swam around in front of and circled
the boat and chittered a greeting.
It was three hours past sunrise.
James Taylor was in the kitchen galley, making toast, strawberry
jam, Coke, and coffee for all three of them, plus Micki Jagger.
Micki Jagger, who had his own sailboat, had flown over to Newport
Beach from Hawaii to sail with them.

Prince Will from England and Harry were also sailing with them, as were Santana and Cindy Blackman Santana, the drummer, and Bruce Springsteen.

Bob Dylan and Prince Will came into the galley and got toast and coffee going for Santana, Cindy, and Harry.

Nederlander 1 was in the crow's nest, acting as a lookout for islands or ocean ships.

Nederlander called to Mikey, who was climbing around on the rigging, "Land ho! I found land, Mikey!"

"Good show, Nederlander," Mikey, the Nederlander executive, called back.

Bobbee brought toast, strawberry jam, and a Coke to Franny and for himself on a tray.

They enjoyed the ocean.

"Thanks, Bobbee," Franny said.

"No problem," Bobbee said.

The land Nederlander had found was Catalina Island, near Los Angeles and Newport Beach, California.

*   *   *

Bruce Springsteen, Bob Dylan, and Prince Will adjusted the mainsail.

Prince Will, Bobbee, Franny, Bruce, Harry, Micki Jagger, and the rest sailed around Catalina Island.

The island was beautiful.

Bruce, Prince Will, Harry, Bobbee, Franny, Mikey, Micki Jagger, Nederlander, and everyone sailed around the island.

Bobbee and Bruce adjusted the spinnaker.

They had lunch on Catalina Island.

They took a picnic from the restaurant for later, and they sailed into a cove. "This is far out," Bob Dylan said.

"Yeah, Bobbee, I love you. I love you as a friend, Bruce and Prince Will, and all of you," Franny said. "This was a great idea." They all loved her as a friend. Bobbee loved Franny.

*   *   *

Clint Eastwood was camping in a big cave in the Catalina Island cove.

Prince Will and Bob Dylan noticed him when they went for a walk to gather firewood and decided to have dinner with him.

Bruce Springsteen and Franny were placing potatoes wrapped in foil in a BBQ ring to bake when Bob Dylan and Prince Will got back with the wood.

Clint was camping with his nephew, Paul.

As Clint was fishing in the stream near the cave, Paul came up from where they had parked the van, lugging the big tent.

"I would have helped you with that," Clint said.

"It's OK. I got it," Paul said, dropping it in a likely spot.

Clint put his fishing pole aside. "Let's put it up."

"You know I didn't want to sleep in no cave," Paul joked.

Clint chuckled. "Wasn't going to. I just wanted to know what you'd say."

The sea breeze added to the atmosphere.

Bobbee, Bruce, and everyone all helped get the big tent erected.

Clint and Paul had put it right beside their little BBQ grill.

The harbor below the cliffs was inviting in appearance.

Prince Will skyped King Charles in England, who liked Prince Will's camping picnic with his friends, including Bobbee Dylan.

Chapter 1A

One day Franny went over to Lizzy's sail-making building on Catalina Island. Captain Bobbee went with Franny.

They found Lizzy making a sail.

Franny said, "Lizzy, this is Captain Bobbee. Bobbee, tell Lizzy about some of the places you've sailed. OK?"

"Happy to meet you," Captain Bobbee said.

"The same, Captain Bobbee," Lizzy said.

"I've been to Europe—all over the coasts there. I've been to Hawaii many times. And Australia, land of the kangaroos and cool people," Captain Bobbee said.

"Wow," Lizzy said. "What did you do in Australia?"

"Holed up along the beaches," Captain Bobbee said. "Went to parties. Docked my ship in some of the marinas."

"That's great," Lizzy said.

"Lizzy, want to come along for a ride? We're going to Hawaii next week," Captain Bobbee asked.

"Sure," Lizzy said. "Right, Franny?"

"Sure," Franny said. "How long a sail?"

"About a month," the captain said. "Leave late morning next Thursday and come back in about a month."

"Sure, I guess I can arrange that," Lizzy said. "I've never been on a long sail before."

"Well, now's your chance," Captain Bobbee said. "I'd love to give you a chance for a long sail."

*   *   *

Bobbee and Franny met Captain Micki Jagger and Prince Will soon after, and everyone loved Bob Dylan's and Micki Jagger's songs, and Lizzy kept asking Bobbee and Micki Jagger questions and commenting on the rock songs.

They all loved "Come In Through My Window" and "Everybody Must Get Stoned," and all Bobbee Dylan's songs and all of Micki Jagger's and Bruce Springsteen's and Santana's and Cindy Blackman Santana's songs.

"When are we going sailing to Hawaii next week?" Clint Eastwood asked Captain Bobbee.

"Be here at 11:00 next Thursday," Captain Bobbee said.

"We'll all be there," Micki Jagger, Bruce Springsteen, and Lizzy said.

Captain Bobbee and everyone were happy with the sailing trip.

Chapter 2

Bobbee Dylan and Bruce Springsteen scanned page 240 in the *Novel & Short Story Writer's Market*.

In there was listed *Hawai'i Pacific Review*.

"The editor is Tyler McMahon, the managing editor is Christa Cushon," Bobbee Dylan said to Bruce Springsteen.

"It's the online literary magazine of Hawai'i Pacific University," Bruce Springsteen said. "It's for authors from Hawaii, the mainland, and elsewhere."

"I know it'll take Francie," Bob Dylan said. "The word length is—"

"Up to four thousand words," Bruce Springsteen said.

"I know Franny's *Sailing* manuscript is unusual and insightful and has cool characters we know she knows," Bob Dylan said.

"You're right, Bobbee," Bruce Springsteen said. "Let's go visit them."

"OK," Bobbee Dylan said.

*　*　*

Hawai'i Pacific University had a cool layout.

Bobbee and Bruce had Easter dinner at the snack bar, which was prepared to the students' wishes.

Bruce and Bobbee lounged around, then went over to the sailboat rental place, which was open 10–6.

They selected a sleek white, brown, and green sailboat and jumped aboard.

Bobbee had contacted Tyler, and soon the magazine editor, and his managing editor, Christa, met them at the boat.

Prince Will motioned from across a bridge and had come to Hawai'i to surprise them. Prince Will loved Bob Dylan and Bruce Springsteen, and they loved him and sailing.

Tyler had an online issue of *Pacific Hawai'i Review* with an article about "Advice From Bob Dylan and Bruce Springsteen For Rockers," and a cartoon illustration from their friend Franny.

Bobbee, Bruce, Prince Will, Tyler, and Christa sailed over to Tyler's cottage and spent the day.

Chapter 3

In Hawaii, Lizzy was strolling through the International Market Place.

Lizzy met two of Prince Will's gentlemen at the sandal shop in the International Marketplace, and they started talking.

"Are you free tomorrow morning?" one asked Lizzy.

"Sure. I don't go to work till 3:00," Lizzy said.

"Maybe Buckingham Palace guards could slip by your hotel or apartment at 10:00 exactly and take you to a royal meeting for the Hawaiian public to meet Prince Will of England," one of the English gentlemen said. "We're Prince Will's staff. We can coordinate right here if you like."

"Sure, that'd be great," Lizzy said. "Kris, my boyfriend, picks me up at 7:00."

"Where's that?" the English gentleman said.

"A sailmaking shop on Ala Moana Boulevard," Lizzy said.

The next morning, Lizzy and Kris were met by the Buckingham Palace guards at 10:00, and Lizzy and Kris were driven to a stop in front of a hotel. As promised, a short line awaited.

"Oh, you'll have to curtsey and bow," the English gentlemen told Lizzy and Kris.

"Curtsey? I'm wearing slacks. How can I do that?" Lizzy asked.

"You can do it," the gentleman said. "Here, I brought a Dame to show you."

Lizzy practiced for fifteen minutes until all were satisfied.

"Ladies and gentlemen, Prince Will of England," a British tone announced.

The short receiving line moved slowly as Prince Will met the Hawaiian public.

Lizzy was presented.

"I'm very pleased to meet you," Prince Will said to Lizzy and Kris. "And you are?"

"I'm Lizzy, and this is my boyfriend, Kris," Lizzy said. "I work at a sailmakers shop here, and I met two of your British team at the International Marketplace by the sandal shop, and they invited me here to meet you."

"Yes, I discovered that story at tea yesterday," Prince Will said. Prince Will said hi to Lizzy and Kris. Then he nodded to a Buckingham Palace guard.

He stepped forward and gave Lizzy and Kris a flyer.

"As you can tell," Prince Will said, "Tomorrow afternoon, we're giving speeches. You two are invited if you want to come. Here are two tickets."

"We'll be there," Lizzy said. "Right, Kris?"

"Absolutely. It's great to meet you again, Prince Will," Kris Kristofferson said. "You know Bob Dylan, I believe. He's next in line. Bob Dylan loves you as a friend, Prince Will, and all of you," Kris Kristofferson said.

"Hello, Bob Dylan. We love you as a friend too," Prince Will said. "I guess we'll find you at the meeting tomorrow. For once, you'll be visiting us backstage." Prince Will chuckled. Bob Dylan chuckled too.

"See you there, Prince Will," Kris Kristofferson said. "Thanks for the event tickets."

Bob Dylan stepped up to talk further with Prince Will.

Lizzy and Kris moved down the line and were happy the English were cordial and charming to Lizzy and Kris.

Kris Kristofferson, Bob Dylan, and Lizzy went to a nearby sidewalk cafe, where they were joined about an hour later by a very incognito Prince Will in a red T-shirt and jeans.

Prince Will had finished the event, and they all went over to join a lavish reception in a Hawaii hotel that looked like a castle.

Chapter 4

Prince William sailed toward Hawaii from Los Angeles, over the rippling blue ocean, planning on going back to meet King Charles, Bob Dylan, Franny, and Bruce Springsteen.

Tyler, Christa, and Bob Dylan were among the first of the group to note the sleek purple and red sailboat.

Bob Dylan called to King Charles, "Hearketh! Prince Will's sailboat cometh!"

"My son," King Charles said affectionately.

Prince William loved to go sailing.

King Charles whirled and danced, and Prince Will sailed around in circles.

Bruce Springsteen and Bob Dylan wrote a song on Prince William's latest adventure.

The docks in Hawaii were inviting, and Prince William eased in skillfully and got the seacraft moored successfully.

Prince William wore a purple and white striped T-shirt and white shorts.

King Charles wore a red polo shirt and navy jeans.

Bobbee Dylan and Bruce Springsteen wore designer shirts with different palm trees and beaches, jeans, and sandals.

"Let's go over to the Hawaii Marina Cafe and interview King Charles, Prince Will, Bob Dylan, and Bruce Springsteen," Christa, managing editor, said.

"OK. Come on, everybody, OK?" Tyler, the editor, said.

"I'll do an interview too," Franny said.

"Lovely idea," King Charles said. "Right, Bobbee and Bruce and Prince Will?"

"Wonderful idea," Bob Dylan, Bruce, and Prince Will said.

"Let's get it on!" Bob Dylan and Bruce Springsteen said.

The Marina Cafe was dancing with activity.

Chapter 5

Bob Dylan, Franny, and Bruce Springsteen were sailing off the coast of Oahu, Hawaii.

"Bobbee-luv," Franny said to Bob Dylan.

"I like that nickname, Franny," Bob Dylan said and kissed her. Franny kissed Bobbee Dylan.

Bob Dylan said, "Hawaii has legal recreational marijuana now—eighteen states do. Plus, Washington, DC. President Joe Biden wants to decriminalize recreational marijuana, and Vice President Kamala Harris wants to legalize marijuana all over the US. And she wants President Joe Biden to help her, according to *Marijuana* magazine."

"Yeah, that'd be really cool," Bruce Springsteen said.

Bobbee Dylan disappeared and came back in a wet suit.

"I'm going to go deep-sea diving a little. Who wants to join me?" he asked.

"I will," David Crosby and Bruce Springsteen said.

"I'll record you getting on and off the boat and swimming in the ocean," Franny said.

Chapter 6

A glamorous moonlit night heralded the sailboat cruise Bobbee and Bruce enjoyed while in Hawaii.

It was the second sailboat cruise they had enjoyed while in the mystical, magical world of Hawaii.

Bruce and Bobbee had set out on the cruise at 7:00 p.m.; it was a very friendly cruise.

The captain and staff played "get acquainted" games with the cruise passengers.

The waves were pointed out by Bruce Springsteen and some of the other moonlight cruise passengers.

Bobbee drank Hawaiian guava juice while Bruce enjoyed wine.

Photographs with the captain and enjoying the ocean view were taken with each guest. Bobbee and Bruce had them taken individually and together, chatting with the captain.

At midnight, Bobbee Dylan phoned Franny. The cruise ended at 12:30 a.m.

Chapter 7

"Baby, I love the beach—Hawaii beach," Bob Dylan said to Franny as he, she, and Bruce Springsteen went down to the beach just after sunrise.

Bobbee, Franny, and Bruce were sitting on three beach chairs, observing the surfers.

"There are several big races across the ocean," Bobbee said. "The two biggest are the Olympics and America's Cup."

"I also discovered there's a Hawaii-to-England race in several weeks, through the Panama Canal and up the Atlantic to the North Sea and ending in London," Bruce said.

"Bruce, I've got to be in that race," Bobbee said. "We ought to be in it. Take Micki Jagger and Santana and James Taylor, and Prince Will."

"That's far out, Bobbee," Bruce said. "There's going to be about twenty-five boats in the race. We can find out more at the Marina Cafe or the university."

"Or the sailboat rental place," Bobbee said. "Let's go this afternoon."

"Sure, Bobbee," Bruce said.

*   *   *

Bobbee and Bruce went up to the *Hawai'i Pacific Review* at the Hawaii Pacific University.

"Hi," Tyler greeted them. "What's up?"

"We're just finding out about racing," Bobbee Dylan said. "We discovered there's going to be a Hawaii-to-England race from Hawaii in several weeks. Have you any knowledge of it?"

"Yeah, here's a notice of it," Tyler said, scanning a folder of *Events*. "Sign up at the boat club on campus. Are you guys going?"

"We're considering it," Bobbee said.

"Cool. How exciting," Christa said. "Wish I could go."

"Maybe you guys can go with us," Bobbee said. "I'd have to get a sailboat. Wanna come?"

"Sure," Christa said.

"It's summer, so we can go," Tyler said.

"I know where there's a boat for sale," Tyler said. "Wanna go look at it this afternoon?"

"Sure," Bobbee said.

"That'd be great," Bruce said.

"Come on then. We've just finished an issue and sent it in," Tyler said.

Tyler drove them all to the Marina and parked to the side was an eighty-foot sailboat.

Bobbee, Bruce, Tyler, and Christa boarded it.

"Seems OK for all of us," Bobbee said.

"Yeah, there's a cabin, galley, five-bedroom cubbies, and a dormitory in it," Bruce said. "The cabin has its own captain's sleeping area curtained off behind the galley."

"Cool," Bobbee said.

The owner came up from below. "You guys want to take a test ride to try her out?"

"Sure," Bruce said.

"Why not?" Bobbee said.

Micki Jagger and James Taylor were coming up the docks to the boat as they began to head out.

"Ahoy, mates!" Micki Jagger said to them, and Micki Jagger and James Taylor came on the cruise too.

It was one whale of an afternoon.

Chapter 8

Franny wanted to give Bob Dylan a gift.

She, Mikey, Bruce Springsteen, and James Taylor went to a large shopping mall in Hawaii.

Franny found a stage outfit. Mikey found new guitar strings. Bruce Springsteen and James Taylor got him a new guitar, custom-made, which Micki Jagger also went in with them to give Bob Dylan. Nederlander got Bobbee a new *Surfing* magazine and a new shirt.

*   *   *

"Do you like to hold me, baby?" Bob Dylan asked.

"Yes," Franny said.

"I like to hold you too," Bobbee said.

Bob Dylan had lots of camaraderie with Franny, and he liked to hold her as she liked to hold him.

*   *   *

"Have you seen my new book, *Santana*?" Santana asked at a coffee shop.

"Your book is great, Santana!" Bob Dylan and Franny said.

"So are yours, Bob Dylan!" Santana said.

They all drank their Cokes and beer.

Mikey, Bruce Springsteen, and the two Nederlanders came in.

Bob Dylan said to Franny, "I love you incredibly."

"And I love you incredibly," Franny said to Bob Dylan.

*   *   *

Bob Dylan leaned on the rail of a sailboat in Hawaii.

Bob Dylan sang his rock song:

And I Would Not Feel So All Alone

Everybody Must Get Stoned!

Prince Will came up to him.

Prince Will was wearing cool brown coveralls with T-straps and a black sweater.

Bob Dylan was wearing a cool striped buttoned shirt with a stripe across the front and each sleeve and shorts.

"I love that song," Prince Will said.

"Thanks. We should be getting to shore pretty soon," Bob Dylan said.

Prince Will was making a documentary on Bob Dylan.

He got the sails and bow in the background, Bob Dylan in the front.

Chapter 9

Bob Dylan stood on stage. His buddies Nederlander 1 and 2, Franny, and Mikey stood in the first row, applauding and cheering.

Bob Dylan and Bruce Springsteen strummed their guitars.

James Taylor and Paul McCartney too came on stage.

The rocker crowd grew quiet.

Bob Dylan said, "Hit it!"

It's a Good World to Get a Break In,
All the Writers & Songwriters Will Be Makin' It
James Taylor is Cool Bruce Springsteen is Cool
Bob Dylan is Cool Paul McCartney is Cool
Santana is cool
And There Will Come a Day
—Everybody Will Get Stoned!

Bob Dylan, Bruce Springsteen, Paul McCartney, James Taylor, and Santana said, "Yeah!"

*   *   *

I'm a Black Magic Concert Giver
I Give Good Concerts For You.
—Santana

Tougher Than the Rest
—Bruce Springsteen

I Wonder If You've Ever
Really Really Really Really
Really
Loved A Woman.
—Bob Dylan

Part 2

Chapter 10

Leaving Hawaii—Race

On Monday morning, a tall sailor, Kris Kristofferson, came running towards the large sailboat up the docks.

Kris Kristofferson raced up the slanting bridge of the ship and said hi to Franny and Bobbee.

"I found Lizzy in the coffee shop and stayed with her a while."

"This is my first mate James," Micki Jagger told Bobbee, captain of his own ship, Franny, Brucie, and Kris K.

"Avast the mainsail!" Micki Jagger said to James.

"Aye, aye!" James said and ran over to adjust the ropes on the mainsail.

On the sailboat ride, Micki Jagger and Bob Dylan had them all talking about boat races.

"We're going to race from Hawaii to England. Wanna come?" Bobbee asked.

"Sure," they all said.

*   *   *

Bob Dylan was captain of the "Bob Dylan." Bruce Springsteen was first mate.

Tori, Wolfgang, Brad, and G. Jagger were on the crew, as were Prince Will, King Charles, Nederlander, Mikey, and Neil Young.

Franny, Tyler, and Christa were journalists.

Micki Jagger was captain of the "Micki Jagger." His crew included Ron Woods and other Jaggers not on Bob Dylan's sailboat—Elizabeth, James, Gabriel, and Georgia-May. The other Jaggers were there to see them off: Liv Tyler, Lucas, Karis, Kim, Jade, and Jasmine.

Santana had his own boat. Cindy Blackman Santana was the first mate, while Fortune, Roddy Ricch, Usher, Lizzy, and Kris Kristofferson were on Santana's crew.

*   *   *

The race to England from Hawaii was on!

Twenty-five boats were strung out from the Hawaii Marina.

The race office sent new data and coordinates for the Panama Canal part of the race of the Pacific Ocean.

The sailboats would speed towards Newport Beach, California, then meander swiftly down the coastline toward the beginning of the Panama Canal.

Just before Newport, Catalina Island would rise into view.

Shore crews and friends could be called any time, no matter the hour, they had told the racers.

Chapter 11

As Bob Dylan's boat sailed over the Pacific Ocean in the lead, TV, news, newspaper, magazine, and radio reporters interviewed him and his first mate, Bruce Springsteen, and the rest of his crew.

Franny, Tyler, and Christa got exclusives to report on race happenings from their boat.

Some TV announcers and *Rolling Stone* said, "What the drama is that people notice on TV or in the media, it stays with them. What is happening to those guys and chicks on the boats—by keeping info clear and non-technical—we can excite and captivate the public."

The boat Bob Dylan got was an eighty-foot sailboat, which had just set a new speed record from California and Florida to England.

Nederlander, Mikey, Franny, and Bruce Springsteen were on Bob Dylan's boat.

Santana's boat had a mostly all-Black crew: First mate Cindy Blackman Santana, Usher, Fortune, Roddy Ricch, Lil Wayne, Lizzy, and Kris Kristofferson.

A network of newspapers gathered on the docks to take stories of the boats' adventures at sea, Bob Dylan, Bruce Springsteen, Santana, and Micki Jagger noted, especially the *Boston Globe*, *New Jersey Times*, and Hawaii publications.

Some held live interviews from their docks with those at sea via Skype, TV, and radio, and *Rolling Stone* joined them.

Magazines and online publications like the *Hawai'i Pacific Review*, *Saturday Evening Post*, *Readers' Digest*, *People*, and *US* flooded to do stories and interviews with the super-stage legend rockers on the boats like Bob Dylan, Bruce Springsteen, Santana, and Micki Jagger about the race.

As the fleet navigated across a large part of the world, adventurous happenings of the sailor rockers racing from Hawaii to England flowed across the United States, Hawaii, and England.

Micki Jagger, Bobbee Dylan, and Bruce Springsteen tracked their race route with experts in Hawaii, California, and England. They "tracked" ocean conditions and considered the two, three, or four most likely scenarios, how they would develop, and how to respond to them.

They passed Catalina Island and pushed on for Newport and the California coast.

They neared the sea opening to the Panama Canal, which took the sailors from the Pacific Ocean to the Atlantic Ocean.

They got through the Panama Canal to the Atlantic Ocean and sailed on the Atlantic towards England.

Bob Dylan's boat stayed in the lead, with Santana's and Micki Jagger's boats close behind.

Prince Will sailed on the "Bob Dylan."

Micki Jagger, Bob Dylan, Bruce Springsteen, and Santana loved a sea captain's advice: "Try to put yourself into a position to get lucky."

As they neared England on the Atlantic to the North Sea, Bob Dylan and Bruce Springsteen knew it was easier for a calm, experienced meteorologist to carefully analyze lots of route maps in an onshore office than for the captain or crew to do it themselves at sea.

Racers used many hours analyzing their intended routes.

The six leaders of the fleet neared the North Sea and nosed in.

Sometime later, Bobbee Dylan docked at a port in London. Bob Dylan had won!

Micki Jagger and Santana tied for second.

Prince Will had everyone's picture taken.

All the sailors were invited to a big party given by King Charles and Prince Will. The party was five days long, just like Bob Dylan,

Bruce Springsteen, the other super-stage legend rockers, Prince Will, and everyone liked.

"What a Fuckin-A party!" Bob Dylan said. Franny, Prince Will, Santana, Bruce Springsteen, Micki Jagger, Tyler, Christa, and Cindy Blackman Santana agreed.

The End

About the Author

Franny Hatch's best friend is Bob Dylan, the super-stage legend rocker.

Franny graduated from Writers Bureau in Manchester, England, and a photography course from Stratford Career Institute in St. Albans, Vermont.

This is her first published book. However, she has had magazine articles published in *Entertainment*, *Purchasing*, *The Sportswoman*, *Orange County Illustrated*, and others.

She has fifteen other stories yet unpublished.

As an illustrator, the author studied illustration for several years in California. Her main and most important teacher was Tom Evans.

When she met Bob Dylan, he and the rock world became a fascination for her.

Made in the USA
Columbia, SC
30 November 2024

48031616R00098